EDUCATION ACT 2002

EXPLANATORY NOTES

INTRODUCTION

1. These explanatory notes relate to the Education Act 2002 which received Royal Assent on 24 July 2002. They have been prepared by the Department for Education and Skills (DfES) in order to assist the reader in understanding the Act. They do not form part of the Act and have not been endorsed by Parliament.

2. The notes need to be read in conjunction with the Act. They are not, and are not meant to be, a comprehensive description of the Act. So where a section or part of a section does not seem to require any explanation or comment, none is given.

3. Abbreviations have been used where appropriate and are explained in the glossary at the end of the notes.

SUMMARY AND BACKGROUND

4. The Education Act implements proposals set out in the White Paper "Schools – achieving success" (Cm 5230) published on 5 September 2001, in five related consultation papers published on the same day ("The Way Forward – a Modernised Framework for School Governance", "Consultation on School Admissions", "Consultation on Exclusion Appeals Panels", "Changes to the Registration and Monitoring of Independent Schools", "Better beginnings – Improving Quality and Increasing Provision in Early Years Education and Childcare") and in a consultation paper issued on 21 September ("16-19 Organisation and Inspection: a Consultation Document"). Implementation in Wales will be guided by the principles set out in the National Assembly for Wales' (NAW) consultation document "The Learning Country" ("Y wlad sy'n Dysgu"), published on 5 September 2001.

Territorial Coverage

5. Except for section 189 and Schedule 17, which amend provisions in the Education Act 1997 (EA 97) which extend to Northern Ireland as well as England and Wales, the Act will extend to England and Wales only.

In general, the provisions have practical application both in England and Wales. There are however some provisions which because of their subject-matter relate only to England or only to Wales.

Part 1: Provision for New Legal Frameworks

6.   This Part makes provision for new legal frameworks in order to support innovation and new forms of service delivery.

Chapter 1 of Part 1: Powers to facilitate innovation

7.   This Chapter introduces a new power for the Secretary of State, or the NAW in Wales, to respond to an application by a qualifying body by issuing an order suspending or modifying legislation for a period of up to 3 years. The power is intended to enable innovative pilot projects to take place and may by order be either extended in time, provided that in total no such project lasts for more than 6 years, or be terminated. The powers set out in this Chapter will last for 4 years.

Chapter 2 of Part 1: Exemptions related to school performance

8.   These provisions will allow, subject to regulations, greater autonomy for governing bodies of qualifying schools over certain elements of teachers' pay and conditions and the national curriculum. The criteria to define qualifying schools, and the specific areas where greater flexibility will be permitted, including which flexibilities will apply by right and which by discretion, will be set out in regulations.

Chapter 3 of Part 1: Powers to form companies etc.

9.   This Chapter enables the implementation of proposals outlined in the policy paper "The Role of the Local Education Authority in School Education" for new models of service delivery. It provides that a school may become a member of a company for the purposes of purchasing goods and providing services for schools and to exercise functions of an LEA, where the LEA chooses to contract them out pursuant to an order under the Deregulation and Contracting Out Act 1994. It also enables the Secretary of State to form or participate in forming companies for purposes connected with her functions relating to education.

Part 2: Financial Assistance for Education and Childcare

10.   This Part makes arrangements for enabling the Secretary of State, or the NAW, to give financial assistance for education and childcare.

11.   At present, the Secretary of State, or the NAW, has a wide variety of powers for making available funding or other forms of financial assistance for purposes connected with education or childcare. This Part repeals many of these powers and replaces them with a single broad power to fund education, childcare and related activities. The assistance may be given through grants, loans, guarantees and incurring expenditure for the benefit

of the person assisted. The power to fund excludes higher education (HE), but includes all other forms of education.

Part 3: Maintained schools

12.   Part 3 makes provisions with respect to the government and financing of maintained schools, and admissions, exclusions and attendance.

Chapter 1 of Part 3: Government of Maintained Schools

13.   This Chapter implements the Government's consultation paper on school governance: "The Way Forward – A Modernised Framework for School Governance".

14.   The Chapter provides that every maintained school shall have a governing body responsible for the conduct of the school with, in accordance with the regulations, an established membership and instrument of government. Regulations will make provisions concerning the control and occupation of school premises by governing bodies. The Chapter introduces measures to enable more than one school to federate under a single governing body, if they so choose, and provided that they comply with prescribed procedures and conditions. In addition, the Secretary of State, or the NAW, may make regulations providing for governing bodies to collaborate by discharging functions jointly either through whole governing bodies or through joint committees.

15.   Provision is made to enable governing bodies to provide community facilities or services for the benefit of their pupils, their pupils' families and the wider community. It also provides for limits to be imposed on those powers. The Chapter also introduces measures requiring governors to produce an annual report; hold an annual parents' meeting; and establish complaints procedures. This Chapter also provides for the staffing of maintained schools, repealing current arrangements and empowering the Secretary of State, or the NAW, to make regulations about the appointment, discipline, suspension and dismissal of staff.

16.   The Chapter also provides that maintained nursery schools are to have governing bodies.

Chapter 2 of Part 3: Financing of Maintained Schools

17.   This Chapter introduces components of a new system for funding LEAs and schools. It introduces new definitions of the 'LEA budget' for central functions and the 'schools budget' for expenditure on pupils. It requires LEAs to establish a schools forum in accordance with regulations, to represent the views of schools with respect to the funding of schools in the area. It also provides a power for the Secretary of State, or the NAW, to

set a minimum level for the schools budget.

18.   In addition, the Chapter provides that the governing body of a maintained school may be required to keep prescribed accounts and records, prepare prescribed financial statements, comply with prescribed audit conditions and to send copies of accounts and financial statements to the Secretary of State or the NAW. Financial statements must also be prepared in relation to private funds.

Chapter 3 of Part 3: Admissions, Exclusions and Attendance

19.   The Chapter makes a number of amendments to the provisions for admission to maintained schools.   It requires LEAs to establish an admission forum to advise on local admissions issues.   It repeals the requirement for schools to have a standard number. It also repeals the power that enables schools with a religious character to agree special arrangements with their LEA for preserving their character. It provides for the Secretary of State, or the NAW, to make regulations requiring LEAs to take action to secure an agreement between admission authorities in the area for co-ordinating admission arrangements. It introduces a power to make regulations with respect to admission appeals.

20.   The Chapter further provides for the exclusion of a pupil from a maintained school, and for regulations to be made in relation to such exclusions, including the procedures to be followed, the arrangements for review of exclusions and appeals against decisions not to reinstate the pupil and adding pupil referral units (PRU) and nursery schools. Provision is also made for the Secretary of State, or the NAW, to require governing bodies to set school-level targets for authorised as well as unauthorised absence.

Part 4: Powers of Intervention

21.   This Part extends the powers through which the Secretary of State, or the NAW, and LEAs may intervene in schools with serious weaknesses or requiring special measures. It introduces a new power to appoint an interim executive board (IEB); and a power for the Secretary of State or the NAW to involve an external partner in turning round a school in special measures or having serious weaknesses.

22.   The Part also extends the powers of the Secretary of State, or the NAW, to intervene in weak LEAs.

Part 5: School Organisation

23.   This Part makes provision about the setting up of new schools and the alteration and discontinuance of existing schools. The first group of sections provides for a new kind of school – the Academy. The second group of sections makes provision about how schools, chiefly maintained

schools, can be established, altered or discontinued. There are changes in who can make proposals for alterations and in the procedures for dealing with proposals.

Part 6: The Curriculum in England

24.   This Part makes provision for a National Curriculum in England, replacing sections 350 to 357 and 362 to 367 of the Education Act 1996 (EA 96), in England. It also re-enacts sections 351 and 352 but with amendments to reflect the incorporation of the foundation stage within the National Curriculum in England.

25.   The Part introduces and provides for the areas of learning within the Foundation Stage. It also separates the first, second and third key stages in England from the fourth key stage and sets out that the National Curriculum shall comprise the attainment targets, programmes of study and assessment arrangements in relation to each key stage. It provides that in relation to the fourth key stage, the Secretary of State may amend the subjects or abolish the Key Stage by order, and re-enacts the special cases provisions of the EA 96.

Part 7: The Curriculum in Wales

26.   This Part separates out the National Curriculum for Wales from that for England. It closely mirrors Part 6, except that it provides for the period and content of the foundation stage to be set out in an order of the NAW and includes the Welsh language in the curriculum.

Part 8: Teachers

27.   This Part makes provision for teachers' pay and conditions, appraisal, qualifications and provision about misconduct. It repeals the School Teachers' Pay and Conditions Act 1991 (STPCA) and replaces its provisions with a modernised framework, but continuing with the main outlines of the existing machinery. It replaces existing requirements for appraisal, and puts in place an updated requirement. It provides for teacher and headteacher qualifications in schools and lecturer and principal qualifications in further education (FE) colleges.

Part 9: Childcare and Nursery Education

28.   This Part deals with childcare and nursery education. In particular it makes provision about the role of LEAs in childcare and nursery education and amends the inspection and registration regimes for childminding and day care and nursery education.

Part 10: Independent Schools

29.   This Part introduces a new regulatory regime, under which independent schools will have to comply with prescribed standards before registration and at all times afterwards. There is also provision about

children with special educational needs (SEN) at independent schools.

Part 11: Miscellaneous and General

30.   This Part imposes a duty on LEAs, the governing bodies of both maintained schools and FE institutions to make arrangements in regard to the welfare of children. It also places a duty on LEAs and the governing bodies of maintained schools to have regard to any guidance from the Secretary of State or the NAW about consultation with pupils in decisions affecting them.

31.   This Part contains provisions relating to education outside schools for 14-16 year olds.

32.   Provision is made to enable the Secretary of State to repay the student loans of those defined by regulations as being eligible.

33.   A number of minor amendments are made to Education Action Zones (EAZs), including an extension to the range of schools eligible to participate and a broadening of the objects of the Zones.

34.   Amendments to inspection provisions include a broadening of the duties of inspectors to report on the management and leadership of schools and a power to enable a member of the Inspectorate to carry out inspections currently only deliverable by a registered inspector.

35.   The powers of the Qualifications and Curriculum Authority (QCA) and the Qualifications, Curriculum and Assessment Authority for Wales (ACCAC) are extended. The powers of LEAs to award qualifications are clarified.

36.   Provision is made to enable regional provision to be made in Wales in respect of children with SEN. A Special Educational Needs Tribunal for Wales is established.

37.   The NAW is given powers to require publication of certain information by schools and LEAs, and to make regulations requiring LEAs in Wales to enter into partnership agreements with schools maintained by them. Provision is also made for the NAW to require the governing bodies of primary and secondary schools to draw up plans together to facilitate the transition of pupils from one to the other.

38.   Amendments are made to the provisions for transport for persons over compulsory school age, to ensure that LEAs develop, publish and implement policies meeting certain criteria. Changes are made to the provisions concerning school meals and milk, to ensure that children not yet of school age receiving funded nursery education may be eligible for free

school meals and milk and that regulations can restrict entitlement to free school meals to children in attendance over the lunch period.

39.   Provision is made making it an offence to create or permit nuisance or disturbance on the premises of a non-maintained special school, an independent school or certain LEA-maintained facilities, and any institution within the further education sector.

40.   The role of the Secretary of State in settling recoupment disputes is ended (although it is retained for the NAW). A power is introduced for the Secretary of State to make payment to the chairmen of local learning and skills councils.

OVERVIEW

41.   The Act is divided into 11 Parts and has 217 sections and 22 Schedules.

42.   Part 1 introduces new legal frameworks, including powers to promote innovation.

43.   Part 2 makes provision for financial assistance, and repeals a significant number of powers to fund education, replacing them with a single general one.

44.   Part 3 makes provision for the governance of maintained schools, replacing Chapter 3 of Part 2 of the School Standards and Framework Act 1998 (SSFA); for the financing of maintained schools, amending Chapter 4 of Part 2 of the SSFA; for the staffing of maintained schools, amending Chapter 5 of Part 2 of the SSFA; for admissions to maintained schools, amending Chapter 1 of Part 3 of the SSFA; and for exclusion of pupils.

45.   Part 4 makes provision for intervention in schools causing concern and LEAs.

46.   Part 5 introduces 'Academies', making changes to the EA 96 and to the Learning and Skills Act 2000 (LSA); and makes changes to provisions for the establishment, alteration and discontinuance of schools in Chapter 2 of Part 2 of the SSFA.

47.   Part 6 replaces for England curriculum provisions in Part 5 of the EA 96.

48.   Part 7 replaces for Wales curriculum provisions in Part 5 of the EA 96.

49.   Part 8 makes provision with respect to teachers, repealing the STPCA and making provision for teachers' pay and conditions, repealing section 218 of the Education Reform Act 1988 (ERA), and making new provision for teachers' qualifications.

50.   Part 9 makes adjustments to provision with respect to nursery education and childcare in the Children Act 1989 (CA) and the SSFA.

51.   Part 10 makes provision with respect to independent schools, and replaces Chapter 2 of Part 7 of the EA 96.

52.   Part 11 makes miscellaneous and general provisions.

COMMENTARY ON SECTIONS AND SCHEDULES

PART 1 – PROVISION FOR NEW LEGAL FRAMEWORKS

Chapter 1 – Powers to facilitate innovation
Sections 1 to 5

Sections 1-5: Powers to facilitate innovation

53.   These sections describe the purpose of this Chapter of the Act which is to facilitate experimental pilot projects in the education system, where the Secretary of State, or the NAW, believes innovation is likely to lead to improvement in educational standards.

54.   These sections require that in forming an opinion as to whether a project may contribute to raising educational standards, the Secretary of State, or the NAW, shall have regard to the need for a school to have a balanced and broadly based curriculum and consider the likely effect of a project on all children who may be affected by it.

55.   The sections allow the Secretary of State, or the NAW, to suspend legislative requirements and, if necessary, modify legislation or confer new powers. The power is limited to education legislation (both primary and secondary). The lifetime of the power is also limited. The power to make entirely new orders will be exercisable only for four years, after which time it is expected that the utility of the power will be reviewed and lessons learnt can be evaluated and disseminated.

56.   No order may be made under these sections if it appears to the Secretary of State, or the NAW, that the proposed order would be likely to have a detrimental effect on the education of children with special educational needs.

57.   The duration of any particular suspension or modification is restricted to three years in the first instance. This provides time for most innovative practices to be implemented and evaluated, while ensuring that pilots remain time limited.

58.   The sections allow orders made under the power to be extended either in scope (both of bodies and functions) or time (subject to a maximum period of six years). It also enables the Secretary of State, or the NAW, to terminate any suspension or modification of legislation. This is to ensure that if it became clear that a specific innovative proposal was not going to deliver the anticipated benefits, the Secretary of State, or the NAW, would be able to reinstate the original legislation.

59.   If any experiment under this power proves worthwhile and the Government is of the view that it should be made permanent, then it would need to consider amending the relevant statutory provisions. It could do so either by way of a Bill to amend the relevant legislation or by way of a Regulatory Reform Order under the Regulatory Reform Act 2001 (c.6).

60.   The sections provide that the effect of a temporary order under the new power may be disregarded for the purposes of section 1(4)(b) of the Regulatory Reform Act 2001 (which prevents the amendment, repeal or replacement of primary legislation through Regulatory Reform Orders within two years of substantive amendment of the relevant provisions). So the restriction in section 1(4)(b) of that Act will not prevent the making of permanent legislative provision in place of the temporary order.

61.   The sections also enable the Secretary of State, or the NAW, to determine the application procedure, and specifically require EAZs and governing bodies of schools maintained by an LEA to consult the relevant LEA as well as requiring the body seeking an order under the power to consult with other appropriate bodies. It also allows the Secretary of State, or the NAW, to change – with the consent of the applicant – the content of the application.

62.   Where the Secretary of State, or the NAW, have made an order under Section 2 they shall prepare a report and in the case of the Secretary of State lay that report before each House of Parliament or publish a report in the case of the NAW.

Chapter 2 – Exemptions related to school performance
Sections 6 to 10

Sections 6 to 10: Exemptions related to school performance

63.   These sections enable any community, foundation, voluntary or special school that is of a prescribed description and satisfies prescribed

criteria to apply for exemption from certain aspects of legislation covering the national curriculum and teachers' pay and conditions.

64.   They enable the Secretary of State, or the NAW, to make regulations specifying the qualifying criteria that a school will be required to meet to be eligible to apply. The application will be to the Secretary of State, or the NAW, for an order to confirm the exemption. Some elements of the pay and conditions and curriculum requirements will be subject to exemption by right, whereas others will be subject to the Secretary of State's, or the NAW's, discretion. The areas in which exemption may apply by right and those in which it will only be available at the discretion of the Secretary of State, or the NAW, will also be set out in regulations.

65.   The governing body of an eligible school will need to consult with appropriate parties, including the LEA, staff within the school and parents, on whether and how to apply. The exemption will apply until such time as the order is revoked or varied.

66.   Revocation or variation can be by order without application if the school has ceased to be a qualifying school.

Chapter 3 – Powers to form companies etc.
Sections 11 to 13

Section 11: Powers of governing bodies to form or invest in companies to provide services etc.

67.   This section provides a new enabling power so that the governing body of a school can form, or take part in forming, companies to purchase goods or provide services for other schools. Such a company could provide, or help with the provision of, facilities or services for schools. It could, for example, provide, or arrange the provision of, the financial, technical and legal advice that schools would normally have to arrange elsewhere, and it could also procure suppliers through the use of standard specifications and contracts.

68.   In addition, maintained schools may form companies to deliver services to any schools on behalf of an LEA, pursuant to a 'contracting out' order under the Deregulation and Contracting Out Act 1994, and/or to provide traded services to schools. The section requires companies to be registered under the Companies Act 1985 as companies limited either by shares or by guarantee.

Section 12: Limits on powers conferred by section 11

69.   This section requires maintained schools wishing to form or join companies established for the purposes of section 11 to obtain the consent of their LEA. Regulations will set out the basis on which an LEA may

refuse consent. Only schools with a delegated budget will be able to belong to such a company.

70.   The section provides for regulations to deal with such matters as the constitution of the company and the effect of the delegated budget being withdrawn from a member school. Companies may not borrow money without consent.

71.   Regulations will put in place arrangements for the financial monitoring of these companies and powers to address any financial mismanagement of the company.

Section 13: General powers of Secretary of State in relation to companies

72.   This section provides for the Secretary of State to form, take part in forming, or invest in a company for purposes connected with her education functions.

PART 2 – FINANCIAL ASSISTANCE FOR EDUCATION AND CHILDCARE

Sections 14 to 18

Sections 14 to 18: Financial assistance for education and childcare

73.   Section 14 enables the Secretary of State or the NAW to give financial assistance for a number of educational or education-related purposes. These purposes are broadly defined and include, among many other objects, childcare, the use of educational buildings for different purposes and the support of teachers. Funds may be directed to schools, LEAs, individuals and companies. Education will include pre-school, school and FE, but not HE (apart from teacher-training). Subsection (2)(a) extends that power beyond the United Kingdom to enable support for visits or international collaboration that would benefit education in England or Wales.

74.   The power allows the Secretary of State, or the NAW, to attach conditions, at her or its discretion, to the provision of assistance. In particular, as well as providing financial assistance directly, section 17 allows financial assistance to be provided via third parties. For example grants might be made available to an LEA, on condition that the LEA passes the grant on to its schools.

PART 3 – MAINTAINED SCHOOLS

Chapter 1 – Government of maintained schools
Sections 19 to 40

Section 19 and Schedule 1: Governing Bodies

75. The section provides for each maintained school to have a governing body which is a body corporate, the constitution and membership of which will be established in accordance with regulations. Currently the SSFA prescribes the membership of governing bodies for different categories of schools.

76. In relation to England, regulations will establish the principles by which schools will be able to set the membership of their governing bodies from certain stakeholder categories and will set proportions to be drawn from them rather than absolute numbers as at present. In voluntary aided schools, foundation governors will be in the majority.

77. The regulations will also establish a single staff governor category to replace separate teacher and non-teacher staff categories and will also establish that within that category one place should be reserved for a teacher, and where at least 3 staff places are available, one place should be reserved for a member of the school's support staff.

78. In relation to Wales the NAW will make the regulations and will consult interested bodies before establishing the requirements for membership and procedures of governing bodies.

79. Regulations under this section will also make provision for other matters relating to the constitution and procedures of governing bodies, including how governors are to be elected or appointed, eligibility, resignation, removal and how governing body meetings should be conducted.

80. This section and the new Schedule 1 replace section 36 of, and Schedules 9, 10 and 11 to, the SSFA. Paragraph 1 of Schedule 10 to the SSFA, which provided for the continuance of governing bodies on the introduction of the new school categories, does not require re-enactment. Schedule 1 re-enacts the rest of that Schedule, with changes that reflect the transfer of functions to the NAW and also the new powers conferred on governing bodies under section 27 to provide community facilities.

Section 20: Instruments of government

81. This section requires every maintained school to have an instrument of government. It also provides the power to establish in regulations the procedures for making, reviewing and varying the instrument of government and its required content.

82. The section replaces section 37 and Schedule 12 of the SSFA. Requirements as to the contents and making of instruments of government,

and their review and variation, will be set out in regulations under this section rather than in Schedule 12 to the SSFA. It is intended that the procedures for making, reviewing and varying instruments of government will be similar to those in Schedule 12, with no change in the requirement for consultation with interested parties.

Section 21: General responsibility for conduct of school

83.   This section re-enacts section 38 of the SSFA. It sets out the governing body's responsibility for the conduct of the school, with an emphasis on promoting high standards. It also provides a power to make regulations on other matters relating to the conduct of the school. In particular, the section re-enacts the existing power to make regulations defining the respective roles and responsibilities of the governing body and the head teacher, but extends it to cover the role and responsibilities of the LEA.

Section 22: Training and support of governors

84.   This section re-enacts without amendment paragraph 7 of Schedule 11 of the SSFA. It provides that the LEA must provide every governor, free of charge, with such information and training as they consider appropriate.

Section 23: Clerk to the governing body

85.   This section re-enacts without amendment paragraph 8 of Schedule 11 of the SSFA. It provides for regulations to make provisions in relation to the clerk of the governing body. Such regulations may include a requirement to appoint a clerk to the governing body or to its committees, the dismissal of the clerk and where the clerk fails to attend, the appointment of a member of the governing body or one of its committees to act as clerk for the purposes of that meeting.

Sections 24 and 25: Federations of schools and supplementary provisions

86.   Section 24 gives effect to the proposal that two or more schools may federate under a single governing body and that the decision to federate should rest with the governing bodies concerned once they have complied with certain conditions and procedures, including consultation with interested parties. Regulations made by the Secretary of State or the NAW may, for example, establish a maximum number of schools that should be able to federate or restrict federation to schools within a certain category or within an individual LEA. Schools within a federation will continue to be treated as individual schools (i.e. that in exercising their duties governing bodies must do so for each school within a federation individually) except in prescribed circumstances.

87.   The section also establishes a power to provide in regulations requirements relating to federations, federated schools and the formation or

dissolution of federations. For example, it is intended to provide for a procedure by which a school within a federation will leave a federation; this may include a requirement to involve the parents of registered pupils at the school.

88.   Section 25 provides that regulations will be able to modify those parts of the SSFA that relate to schools causing concern and financial delegation as to how they should apply to federations. Similarly it provides that the regulations may modify any enactment that relates to different categories of schools as to how those individual schools in, or the governing body of, a federation should be treated.

Section 26: Collaboration between schools

89.   This section provides for regulations to be made that would allow governing bodies to collaborate by arranging for joint discharge of functions either through whole governing bodies or through joint committees. The section permits those governing bodies that wish to collaborate but do not wish to federate under a single governing body, as provided for in section 24, to have the opportunity to form joint committees or hold joint meetings.

Sections 27 and 28: power of governing body to provide community facilities

90.   These sections enable the governing bodies of all maintained schools to provide any facilities or services which will further any charitable purpose for the benefit of their pupils, families of pupils and the wider community. This power is in addition to the governing body's general responsibility to conduct the school with a view to promoting high standards of educational achievement at the school.

91.   These sections give governing bodies flexibility by, for example, allowing them to incur expenditure, enter into agreements and charge for any services or facilities.

92.   Schedule 1 provides that the general powers of the governing body relate to the provision of community facilities as well as the governing body's core duty of provision of education.

93.   The sections place certain limits on governing bodies should they decide to exercise their power. Section 28 provides that governing bodies' power to provide community facilities is subject to any limits or restrictions contained in the school's instrument of government and the local authority's financial scheme under section 48 of SSFA. The sections ensure governors cannot exercise the power to provide community facilities if it interferes with the duties they are required to carry out under Education Acts and contain a power to make regulations to prohibit certain specific

types of service.

94.   The sections require the governing body to consult the LEA, school staff, parents, pupils and any other people the governing body thinks appropriate before exercising this power, to have regard to any guidance issued by the Secretary of State or the NAW and to have regard to any advice offered by the LEA.

Section 29: Additional functions of governing body

95.   The section re-enacts section 39 of the SSFA. It requires governing bodies to establish a procedure to deal with complaints not covered by existing statutory requirements in relation to delivery of the National Curriculum, provision of collective worship and religious education (RE), SEN assessments, admissions and exclusions. In producing their complaints procedures, governing bodies will be required to have regard to any guidance given by the Secretary of State or the NAW. It is intended that the guidance will set out the general principles. The existing regulation-making power in section 39(1) has never been exercised. Unlike section 39(1), section 29(1) will apply to maintained nursery schools.

96.   The section also makes provision for governing bodies to require pupils to attend any place outside the school for curriculum purposes. The section also extends the requirement for the governing body and head teacher of community, community special or voluntary controlled schools to comply with LEA directions in relation to health and safety on the school premises or elsewhere when taking part in school activities to governing bodies of maintained nursery schools.

Section 30: Governors' reports and other information

97.   This section replaces sections 42 and 43 of the SSFA. The section places a duty on governing bodies of maintained schools to produce an annual report and provide for regulations to specify the content and other requirements including those relating to the distribution and availability of the annual report. The Government intends that such regulations will allow governing bodies to combine their annual report with their prospectus should they wish. The section also places a requirement on the governing body to provide the LEA with the information it requires about the discharge of the governors' functions. The head teacher is required to provide the governing body or the LEA with information to enable them to fulfil their statutory functions.

Section 31: Control of school premises

98.   This section replaces section 40 and Schedule 13 of the SSFA. It provides for regulations on the control of the occupation and use of school premises by governing bodies.

Section 32: Responsibility for fixing dates of terms and holidays and times of sessions

99.   This section re-enacts section 41 of the SSFA.   It sets out who is responsible for determining the dates of school terms and holidays as well as the times of school sessions and extends the provision to maintained nursery schools as they are now to have a governing body.

Section 33: Annual parents' meeting

100.   This section requires governing bodies to hold an annual parents' meeting and describes their purpose. Regulations will set out the circumstances under which governing bodies will be exempt from holding such meetings. None of the other provisions in section 41 of the SSFA relating to processes and procedures are being re-enacted.

Section 34: Arrangements for government of new schools

101.   This section re-enacts, with amendments, section 44 of the SSFA. It sets out the arrangements for the governance of new schools before and shortly after they open. The section therefore provides that where proposals for the establishment of a maintained school are approved, the LEA must make arrangement for the constitution of a temporary governing body and that it will exist until a permanent governing body has been constituted. The section requires that a permanent governing body should be constituted after the school opening date and by a time to be specified in regulations. The regulations will allow temporary governing bodies to continue in existence until the changes introduced by the Act come into force. The section also provides that regulations may cover matters relating to the temporary governing body including its meetings and proceedings, payment of allowances and the transition to a permanent governing body.

Section 35: Staffing of community, voluntary controlled, community special and maintained nursery schools

102.   This section contains provisions regarding the staffing of community, voluntary controlled, community special and maintained nursery schools. It replaces the current arrangements set out in section 54 and Schedule 16 of the SSFA, which are repealed. It provides enabling powers for the Secretary of State, or the NAW, to make regulations, supplemented by statutory guidance, related to the appointment, discipline, suspension, and dismissal of staff.

103.   The section provides for LEAs to be the employer of staff in community, voluntary controlled, community special, and maintained nursery schools and for such schools to have a head teacher and enables staff to be engaged to work in these schools otherwise than under a contract of employment.

104.   The section provides for any regulations made under the section to

be replaced by Part 1 of Schedule 2 at any time when a school's delegated budget is suspended by the LEA.

Section 36: Staffing of foundation, voluntary aided and foundation special schools

105. This section contains provisions regarding the staffing of foundation, voluntary aided and foundation special schools. It replaces the current arrangements set out in section 55 and Schedule 17 of the SSFA, which are repealed. It provides enabling powers for the Secretary of State, or the NAW, to make regulations, supplemented by statutory guidance, related to the appointment, discipline, suspension, and dismissal of staff.

106. The section provides for governing bodies to be the main employer of staff in foundation, voluntary aided and foundation special schools, for such schools to have a head teacher and also enables staff to be engaged to work in these schools otherwise than under a contract of employment.

107. The section provides for any regulations made under the section to have effect subject to Part 2 of Schedule 2 at any time when a school's delegated budget is suspended by the LEA.

Schedule 2 Part 1: Effect on staffing of suspension of delegated budget: Community, voluntary controlled, community special and maintained nursery schools

108. Part 1 of this Schedule provides for particular arrangements to come into effect in place of any regulations in relation to the staffing of community, voluntary controlled, community special and maintained nursery schools, at any time when a school's delegated budget is suspended. Subject to consultation with the governing body and the arrangements for the appointment and dismissal of reserved teachers at voluntary controlled schools, the LEA may appoint, suspend and dismiss staff at the school as the authority thinks fit.

Schedule 2 Part 2: Effect on staffing of suspension of delegated budget: Foundation, voluntary aided and foundation special schools

109. Part 2 of this Schedule provides for particular arrangements to come into effect in relation to the staffing of foundation, voluntary aided and foundation special schools, at any time when a schools delegated budget is suspended. It provides for any staffing regulations under section 36 to have effect subject to the LEA having particular rights over the school's staff, the governing body's appointment and dismissal of staff, the educational qualifications of teachers giving secular education, and the conditions of service of persons employed for the care and maintenance of the school premises.

Section 37: Payments in respect of dismissal, etc

110. This section re-enacts the provisions of section 57 of the SSFA

dealing with payments in respect of dismissal of staff from maintained schools, including payments for dismissal and securing the resignation of staff, payments required under contract or statutory provision, and payments for premature retirement. This section only differs from the SSFA provisions in so far as it includes an additional provision related to payments in respect of dismissal of staff employed for community purposes.

111.   This additional provision requires the LEA to recover from the governing body any costs the authority has incurred arising from the premature retirement, dismissal, or in securing the resignation, of staff employed at the school for community or family services. However this subsection allows this requirement to be waived where the authority has agreed with the governors in writing that all or part of the costs will not be recovered in this way. The new parts of this section apply even if the delegated budget is withdrawn.

112.   Where the governing body are required to pay the costs relating to dismissal or premature retirement of a member of staff employed for community purposes they may not do so out of the school's budget share.

113.   Where a member of staff is employed partly for the purpose of the school, say as a classroom assistant, and partly for community purposes, say supporting adult education, the costs must be apportioned between the school's budget share and the funds the school holds for expenditure on community purposes.

114.   Regulations may also be made which provide for the recovery of costs in relation to the dismissal of staff employed for community purposes.

Section 38: Communication with schools

115.   This section requires the Secretary of State and National Assembly when considering whether to issue guidance to have regard to the desirability of providing information about good educational practice, the benefits expected to result from any particular piece of guidance and the desirability of avoiding excessive material. It also imposes a duty on both the Secretary of State and National Assembly to produce an annual report listing all documents sent during the year to maintained schools

Section 39: Interpretation of Chapter 1

116.   This section has the effect of applying to nursery schools the requirements for schools to have legally constituted governing bodies and the majority of the consequent powers, duties and responsibilities invested in those governing bodies. Currently all maintained schools are required to have governing bodies. Nursery schools are schools maintained by LEAs

but are not within the definition of maintained schools in section 20(7) of the SSFA and are therefore not currently captured by this requirement.

117. It is proposed that nursery schools should have similar provisions for establishing governing bodies and making and amending instruments of government, as for maintained schools. As a consequence, nursery school governing bodies will take on similar responsibilities, powers and duties, as for maintained schools, including delegated budget shares, staffing, Ofsted inspection and conduct of the school. It is not proposed to apply admissions legislation fully to nursery schools: the responsibility for making decisions about the admission of a pupil will be dealt with by regulations.

118. The governing bodies of maintained nursery schools will have power to provide community facilities and services.

Section 40: Amendments of Part 2 of School Standards and Framework Act 1998

119. This section introduces Schedule 3 which provides that governing body may not use the school's budget share to finance any services they provide under the new power. The financial management of community services provided by governing bodies may be subject to requirements contained in the financial schemes prepared by LEAs under section 48 of the SSFA.

120. The Schedule also inserts a new section in the SSFA to provide cover by LEAs in cases where a third party has a claim arising from the provision of community services. The LEA may recover these costs from the school. However, these costs cannot be recovered from the school's budget share.

121. Where it appears to an LEA that a governing body are not managing their expenditure on community services satisfactorily, the LEA may suspend the governing body's right to a delegated budget.

Chapter 2 – Financing of maintained schools
Determination of budgets
Sections 41 to 43

Sections 41 to 43: Determination of specified budgets of LEA, power of Secretary of State to set minimum schools budget and Schools Forums

122. These sections are related to the introduction of a new system of funding LEAs and schools in England. Much of this will be accomplished under existing local government finance legislation - the Local Government Finance Act 1992 (as amended). The new system will involve separate financial assessments for expenditure on school pupils and expenditure on the central functions of LEAs. These sections amend education finance legislation to bring it into line and set up new arrangements in connection

with the new system.

123.   Section 41 introduces new definitions of the "LEA budget" for central functions and the "schools budget" for expenditure on pupils. Details will be set out in regulations. That part of the schools budget which is placed under the control of individual schools will continue to be known as the "individual schools budget". These new definitions will apply in Wales but in the context of the existing funding arrangements for LEAs and schools. The Secretary of State, or the NAW, will continue to have power to set limits on the classes, descriptions and amounts of expenditure that may or must be deducted from the schools budget to arrive at the individual schools budget.

124.   Section 41 requires LEAs to notify the Secretary of State, or the NAW, and all the schools maintained by them, by the end of January each year, of the proposed amount of their schools budget for the following financial year. Section 42 provides for a reserve power of intervention by the Secretary of State, or the NAW. It is intended that this would be exercised in exceptional circumstances, where the Secretary of State, or the NAW, considers that the schools budget proposed by the LEA is seriously inadequate. It also allows the Secretary of State to intervene if an authority fails to notify him of its proposed budget by the end of January. In coming to such a conclusion the Secretary of State, or the NAW, would have to consider all relevant circumstances, such as an LEA's proposed schools budget compared with its school funding assessment; the performance of an LEA's schools; significant and demonstrable pressures from other services; or the degree to which the authority has failed to pass on extra funding for schools.

125.   Section 43 requires LEAs to establish a schools forum, to represent the views of schools and such other organisations as are included by the LEA in the membership of the forum, on the authority's schools budget. The functions of the forum will be set out in regulations: it is intended that they will include the giving of advice on funding policy and other financial issues affecting schools, which the LEA will be obliged to take into account in setting the schools budget; consultation on the LEA's school funding formula, and consultation on contracts for services provided by the local authority.

Accounts and financial statements
Sections 44 and 45

Sections 44 and 45: Accounts of maintained schools and financial statements
126.   These sections will allow requirements to be imposed as to the way

maintained schools keep accounts, and report information based upon those accounts. In England, this will be implemented under the Consistent Financial Reporting (CFR) initiative for schools. This will provide a consistent minimum standard for school financial reporting, and enable all schools to compare their expenditure with that of similar schools. The Secretary of State, or the NAW, will publish information reported by schools so as to facilitate financial benchmarking. The main provision will also allow requirements to be imposed as to the way in which maintained schools' resources are to be audited. In both cases the scope of the provision extends both to public funds and private funds controlled by the governing body.

127. Section 45 makes related amendments of section 52 of the SSFA, extending the scope of that section to private funds included in the main provision. This will enable LEAs, in publishing their annual out-turn statements, to include data relating to such funds.

Chapter 3 – Admissions, exclusions and attendance
Admission arrangements
Sections 46 to 51

128. The following sections introduce a number of changes to the current legal framework that instructs LEAs and school governing bodies on how they should operate their school admission arrangements. Guidelines for England are set out in the School Admissions Code of Practice and the School Admission Appeals Code of Practice, in force since April 1999 and September 1999 respectively. Revised versions of these Codes, to reflect the legislative changes, will be issued in January 2003. Guidelines for Wales are set out in corresponding Codes of Practice, which will also be revised.

Section 46: Admission forums
129. This section amends the SSFA by inserting a new section 85A to require LEAs, through regulations, to establish advisory bodies, to be known as admission forums, to discuss and advise on local school admission issues including proposed admission arrangements. It also inserts a new section 85B to require admission forums to advise Academies about local admission arrangements, and requires the governing body of an Academy to have regard to the advice given by the forum. There is provision for LEAs to establish such admissions forums jointly with one or more neighbouring LEAs. This provision replaces the current guidance from the Secretary of State and the NAW in the Codes of Practice on School Admissions that recommends voluntary bodies for this purpose. There will be a requirement on admission forums to advise Academies, as well as maintained schools, and for Academies to have regard to such

advice (see section 66).

Section 47: Admission numbers

130.   This section, together with the relevant repeals, removes the requirement for a school to have a standard number (relating to an age group in which pupils are normally admitted to the school) as regards the number of pupils who are to be admitted in any particular school year. It inserts a new section 89A into to the SSFA, under which admission authorities will have to consider, amongst other factors, the current capacity of the school (as determined under a new formula which is being introduced) when setting an admission number. Section 86(5) of the SSFA is amended so that prejudice to efficient education or the efficient use of resources may not be taken to arise (and, therefore, the duty to comply with parental preference will apply) until such time as an admission authority has admitted the number of pupils it has determined to admit in the year in question. This section also inserts new provisions into the SSFA which allow admission authorities for schools which provide boarding accommodation to have separate admission numbers for their day and boarding places respectively. Under these, day place applicants are to be considered separately from boarding applicants, and vice versa.

Section 48: Co-ordination of admission arrangements

131.   This section amends the SSFA by inserting new sections 89B and 89C which allow regulations to be made requiring LEAs to co-ordinate, for their areas, school admission arrangements as between themselves and those maintained schools which are responsible for their own admissions. The effect is that LEAs must attempt to negotiate agreement between all maintained schools in their area for a co-ordinated application process for local parents. Each LEA will be responsible for the administration of the co-ordinated arrangements. Regulations may also require that all parents in an LEA's area are made an offer of a school place on the same day. If an LEA and other admission authorities are unable to agree a scheme, the Secretary of State, or (in Wales) the NAW, will have the power to impose one. The NAW will have the same regulation-making power in relation to Wales.

Section 49: Repeal of power to make certain special arrangements for preserving religious character

132.   This section repeals section 91 of the SSFA which allows foundation or voluntary aided faith schools to make special arrangements to preserve their religious character.

Section 50: Admission Appeals

133.   This section amends section 94 of the SSFA to reflect the repeal of Schedule 24, relating to admission appeals, which will be replaced by

regulations.

134.   Admission appeal panels consider parents' appeals against the decision of an LEA or governing body (where it is the admission authority for a school) to refuse their child a place. The current provisions that govern arrangements by LEAs and schools for such appeals, and their operation, will in future be prescribed by regulations.

Section 51: Further amendments relating to admission arrangements

135.   This section introduces Schedule 4 which contains a number of other amendments to statutory provisions relating to school admission arrangements, as follows.

136.   The definition of "appeal panel" in section 84(6) of the SSFA is amended to reflect the substitution of the provisions of Schedule 24 by regulations.

137.   Section 86 of the SSFA is further amended to clarify that a parent may express more than one preference for the school they wish their child to attend, to which the duty to comply placed on LEAs and governing bodies by subsection (2) will apply. Provision is also made to clarify that this duty also applies in relation to preferences expressed for a school's sixth form.

138.   Section 87, which removes the requirement from LEAs and school governing bodies to comply with a parent's request to admit their child if he or she has been permanently excluded from two or more schools, is amended. The effect is that a child is not to be regarded as having been permanently excluded from a school for the purposes of section 87 if, had it been practical to do so, either a governing body reviewing the head teacher's decision to exclude or an exclusion panel hearing an appeal against the governing body's refusal to direct reinstatement, would have directed that the child be reinstated.

139.   Section 89 of the SSFA, which sets out the procedure for determining admission arrangements annually, is amended. The main change is to provide governing bodies of community and voluntary controlled schools with a right to be consulted about the admission arrangements which admission authorities for other schools in their areas propose to make. This, in turn, will give such governing bodies the right to refer objections about proposed admissions arrangements to the Schools Adjudicator, or the NAW, to the extent permitted by regulations. Admission authorities may also be required to publish their proposals in certain circumstances, such as where they intend to admit fewer pupils than the school has capacity for (as calculated under a formula); this is for the purpose of enabling (by regulations) groups of ten or more parents to refer

an objection to the Schools Adjudicator about the proposed admission number.

140.   In addition, where the admission authority is a school's governing body, the new section 89(2A) allow for regulations to provide that the duty to consult may be disapplied in certain circumstances (for example, where their admission arrangements have not been the subject of previous objection to the Schools Adjudicator and remain unchanged).

141.   Section 90 of the SSFA is amended to clarify that an objection about proposed admission arrangements can be referred to the Schools Adjudicator, or (in Wales) the NAW, by anyone in the local area who should have been consulted about them, even if they were not.

142.   A new section 92 of the SSFA is substituted, enabling information requirements to be placed in regulations.

143.   Section 94 is further amended to clarify that any refusal to transfer a pupil already admitted to a secondary school into that school's sixth form carries the right of appeal. Section 95 of the SSFA is amended to reflect the repeal of Schedule 25 in relation to the making and hearing of appeals by governing bodies of community and voluntary controlled schools against an LEA's decision (where it is the admission authority) to admit to that school a child who has been permanently excluded from two or more schools. The provision presently contained in Schedule 25 to the SSFA is now to be made by regulations.

144.   Sections 96 and 97, which relate to the power LEAs have to direct a school to admit a child who has been refused admission to, or permanently excluded from, every other suitable school within a reasonable travelling distance of the child's home, are amended. They clarify that such a direction may only be given to a school for which the LEA is not the admission authority. They also clarify that where (following a referral) the Secretary of State, or the NAW, decides that the child should be admitted to a different school for which the LEA is the admission authority, the LEA must admit the child to that school.

145.   Section 98 of the SSFA is amended to clarify which of the LEA or the governing body of a maintained school has responsibility for any decision relating to the admission of a child to a nursery class at such a school. Provision is also made for regulations to make such provision in relation to maintained nursery schools.

146.   Section 3 of the Diocesan Boards of Education Measure 1991 is amended to require an admission authority for a Church of England school to consult the Diocesan Board about its proposed admission arrangements

before going out to the statutory consultation with other admission authorities.

Exclusion of pupils
Section 52

Section 52: Exclusion of pupils

147.   Subsections (1) and (2) of this section, which give head teachers of maintained schools power to exclude any pupil from the school on disciplinary grounds and gives the same power to teachers in charge of PRUs, re-enact the existing provisions in section 64(1) of the SSFA and paragraph 7 of Schedule 1 to the EA 96.

148.   The rest of the section provides for the procedures relating to the exclusion of pupils, including the arrangements for reviewing exclusions and appealing against decisions not to reinstate the pupil in question, to be set out in regulations. It is intended that the existing requirement for head teachers, governing bodies, LEAs and appeal panels to have regard to the Secretary of State's, or the NAW's, guidance relating to exclusion will be continued under those regulations.

149.   Under the proposed regulations, the procedures for excluding a pupil from a maintained school other than a PRU will be largely unchanged. It is proposed, however, that regulations may provide for altering the constitution of the appeal panel; ensuring that, when reaching a decision, panels will be required to consider the interests of the whole school community, not just those of the excluded pupil; and for ensuring that defects in prior procedure will not alone constitute grounds for reinstating a pupil.

150.   Regulations may also provide for changes to the number of days a fixed period exclusion must be before the governing body, through its discipline committee, is required to review it.

151.   In relation to PRUs, the section provides the parent of a pupil permanently excluded from a PRU a right to appeal equivalent to that available to the parents of pupils excluded from maintained schools. The right will be given retrospectively to 1st September 1994, the date when PRUs were first recognised in statute.

152.   The section also adds maintained nursery schools to the exclusions regime.

Attendance targets
Section 53

Section 53: Attendance targets

153.   Section 63 of the SSFA enables the Secretary of State or the NAW to require school governing bodies to set school-level targets for unauthorised absence. Unauthorised absences are absences that have not been approved by the school. The section extends this power to include authorised absence and will therefore enable the Secretary of State, or the NAW, to require specified schools to set targets to reduce their overall level of absence.

PART 4 – POWERS OF INTERVENTION

Schools causing concern
Sections 54 to 59

Section 54: Duty to notify where inspection shows school causing concern

154.   The section inserts a new provision as section 16A in the School Inspections Act 1996 (SIA) to place a duty on HMCI to notify the Secretary of State, or the NAW, where an inspector has concluded that a school has serious weaknesses or requires special measures. This change enables other provisions of this Part to allow earlier intervention by the Secretary of State, or the NAW, or by LEAs in such schools.

155.   The section identifies the routes by which HMCI might be notified, whether by one of Her Majesty's Inspectors (HMI) or by a registered inspector, that a school has been judged to have serious weaknesses or to require special measures. It provides that HMCI must agree with a registered inspector that a school requires special measures.

156.   The section requires HMCI to notify the Secretary of State, or the NAW, in writing that a school requires special measures or has serious weaknesses; and requires the Secretary of State, or the NAW, to notify the relevant LEA in writing that she has been informed of that judgement in respect of a named school. The section defines when a school is to be regarded for this purpose as having serious weaknesses. 'Special measures' is defined in the SIA.

Section 55: Cases in which powers of intervention exercisable

157.   The section amends section 15 of the SSFA by replacing the subsections which define when the section applies to schools having serious weaknesses or requiring special measures. This change ensures that the steps taken by the Secretary of State, or the NAW, or by LEAs to secure improvement in such schools can commence more quickly after an inspection has reached such a conclusion.

158.   The section provides that section 15 applies to a school having

serious weaknesses when, following an inspection of that school, the Secretary of State, or the NAW, is notified in writing of the inspector's opinion, as required in section 54, (and no subsequent inspection has concluded that the school no longer has serious weaknesses or that the school requires special measures).

159.   The section provides that section 15 applies to a school requiring special measures when, following an inspection of that school, HMCI notifies the Secretary of State, or the NAW, in writing of this judgement (and no subsequent inspection has concluded that the school no longer requires special measures).

Section 56: Power of the Secretary of State to appoint additional governors or direct closure

160.   The section amends sections 18 and 19 of the SSFA so as to extend the powers currently available to the Secretary of State, or the NAW, to intervene in schools requiring special measures to those identified by HMCI as having serious weaknesses. It provides that the Secretary of State, or the NAW, may appoint additional governors and appoint one of those governors as chair of the governing body or may direct the maintaining LEA to discontinue (close) on a specified date a school which requires special measures or has serious weaknesses.

Schedule 5: Amendments consequential on sections 55 and 56

161.   This Schedule amends existing legislation resulting from the changes proposed in sections 55 and 56, making changes to sections 14, 16 and 17 of the SSFA.

162.   It amends section 14(3), so that LEAs may not use their powers in sections 16 and 17 to appoint additional governors and/or suspend a school's right to a delegated budget if the Secretary of State, or the NAW, has used the powers under sections 18 and 19 to appoint additional governors or direct an LEA to close a school, where a school requires special measures or has serious weaknesses.

163.   It amends section 16 to allow an LEA to exercise their power to appoint additional governors for schools requiring special measures or having serious weaknesses: ten calendar days after the Secretary of State, or the NAW, has given notice to the LEA required by section 46.

164.   It allows appropriate appointing authorities in voluntary aided schools to appoint additional governors from the same stage where a school is in special measures or has serious weaknesses, provided the Secretary of State, or the NAW, has chosen not to do so and to appoint an equal number of additional governors to those appointed by LEAs when a school has been

placed under a formal warning.

165.   It amends section 17 to allow an LEA to exercise its power to suspend a school's delegated budget at the same stage when a school requires special measures or has serious weaknesses.

Section 57: Power of LEA to provide for governing body to consist of interim executive members

166.   This section provides the LEA with an additional power to appoint a specially constituted governing body in place of the pre-existing governors.

167.   This power may be exercised only with the consent of the Secretary of State, or the NAW. The governing body must be given written notice of the exercise of the power. The section sets out the circumstances in which the LEA may exercise the power.

168.   Before using the power the LEA must consult the governing body of the school; in the case of a church school, foundation or voluntary, the appropriate diocesan authority; and in the case of any other foundation or voluntary body those who appoint the foundation governors.

Section 58: Power of Secretary of State to provide for governing body to consist of interim executive members

169.   This section enables the Secretary of State, or the NAW, to appoint a specially constituted governing body.

170.   The section places a duty on the Secretary of State, or the NAW, before exercising the power, to consult the LEA; the governing body of the school; in the case of a church school, foundation or voluntary, the appropriate diocesan authority; and in the case of any other foundation or voluntary body those who appoint the foundation governors. The consultation need not take place if the LEA has already consulted them in connection with a proposal to use its powers under section 16A.

Section 59: Governing Bodies consisting of interim executive members

171.   This section inserts a new section 19A in SSFA and provides for the Schedule set out as Schedule 6 to the Act to become a new Schedule 1A to SSFA.

Schedule 6: Governing Bodies consisting of interim executive members – to be inserted in the School Standards and Framework Act as Schedule 1A

172.   This Schedule contains detailed provisions relating to the temporary replacement of the normally constituted governing body of a school with a specially constituted governing body consisting of interim executive members. The governing body remains in existence as a body corporate, but its membership is changed. The specially constituted governing body is

referred to in the Schedule as an "interim executive board" (IEB), but it will run the school as "the governing body of ..... School" and will have the responsibilities of a governing body.

173.   The Schedule allows current members of the governing body to be appointed; provides for the number of interim executive members to be two or more; enables further members to be appointed at any time; requires the LEA or Secretary of State, or the NAW, to consult appropriate interests before appointing members. The Schedule provides that members can be removed for incapacity or misbehaviour; allows the duration of the interim period to be specified; provides for the LEA or Secretary of State, or the NAW, to nominate one member as chairman and for interim executive members to be paid. It also provides for the IEB to determine its own procedures; exempts it from regulations relating to normal governing bodies; and provides for the school's instrument of government not to be applied.

174.   The Schedule explains that during the interim period when the IEB is in place the LEA will not be able to use its usual powers to appoint additional governors and/or suspend a school's right to a delegated budget. The Secretary of State, or the NAW, will also lose the power to appoint additional governors when an IEB is in place.

175.   An IEB will not have the power to publish proposals to close a school, if it concludes that a school cannot be turned around. It will be able to report recommending that a school should be closed to the LEA and the Secretary of State, or the NAW.

176.   The interim period and the appointment of the IEB may continue until the date of closure when the Secretary of State, or the NAW, or the LEA use their powers of closure or direction to close in SSFA. The LEA or the Secretary of State, or the NAW, is given the ability to specify in a notice a date on which a normally constituted governing body will return to the school.

177.   The Schedule sets out when interim executive members will leave office, either when a school closes or where the duration of an interim period is specified, the last day, or where a notice is given for the restoration of a normally constituted governing body, the date specified. It provides for an LEA to make arrangements for the constitution of the normal governing body and enables regulations to be made for a shadow (transitional) governing body to be established and governors to be elected or appointed before the end of the interim period.

Local education authorities
Sections 60 to 64

Section 60: Powers of Secretary of State to secure proper performance of LEA's functions

178.   The new section 497A(1) for the EA 96 enables the Secretary of State, or the NAW, to give directions in relation to all education functions, including for example those relating to early years education, rather than at present only those relating to compulsory age education. Section 497A(2A) enables the Secretary of State, or the NAW, to give a further direction when one direction comes to an end and she is not satisfied that the authority would perform the functions to an adequate standard were they to be taken back in-house.

179.   Section 497A(4) as substituted enables the Secretary of State, or the NAW, to direct LEAs to take more specific action without the setting of objectives as presently required. This is in line with powers in section 15 of the Local Government Act 1999, which enable the Secretary of State, or the NAW, to take any action considered necessary or expedient to secure an authority's compliance with its duties. Section 497A(4A) enables the Secretary of State, or the NAW, to direct that a function is to be exercised by the Secretary of State, or the NAW, or by a nominee.

Section 61: Power to secure proper performance: duty of authority where directions contemplated

180.   This section inserts in the EA 96 a new section 497AA which provides that when the Secretary of State, or the NAW, is satisfied that an authority is failing to perform its statutory functions to an adequate standard, and has notified the authority of her decision to intervene, and to whom the right of access granted by this section should apply.   The authority is then obliged to give full co-operation to the nominee, rather than such a duty only arising after a direction is given under section 497A.

Section 62: Power to secure proper performance: further provisions

181.   Section 497B is amended to take account of the amendments to the section 497A. In addition, the new section 497B (1A) defines to whom the general rights conferred by section 497B apply. Following a direction by the Secretary of State, or the NAW, that person is the contractor or nominee of the Secretary of State or the NAW.

Section 63: Power to require LEA to obtain advisory services

182.   This section enables the Secretary of State, or the NAW, to direct an LEA to involve an external partner in providing advice to the LEA or the governors of a maintained school (or both). The power to direct applies when the LEA in question maintains at least one school which requires special measures or has serious weaknesses: and in addition it appears to the Secretary of State that the LEA has not made or is unlikely to make sufficient progress in eliminating such failings in such a school or schools,

or is unlikely to eliminate such failings as may be found in the future in other schools it maintains, or has a disproportionate number of such schools. External partners could be successful schools, successful LEAs, FE or HE institutions, or from the public, voluntary or private sectors.

Section 64: Provisions supplementary to section 63

183.   This section gives supplementary powers to the Secretary of State, the NAW or an external partner and requires an LEA to whom a direction under section 63 is or may be given to provide assistance.

PART 5 – SCHOOL ORGANISATION

Academies and city colleges
Sections 65 to 69

Section 65 and Schedule 7: Academies

184.   Section 482 of the EA 96, as originally enacted, made provision for the setting up of schools known as city technology colleges (CTCs) and city colleges for the technology of the arts (CCTAs). These are independent secondary schools with private sponsors which receive funding from central government. As their names suggest they have a particular subject emphasis and are situated in urban areas.

185.   That section was amended by the LSA to allow for a further category of secondary school – city academies. These schools were based on a similar model to CTCs, but could have a curriculum emphasis drawn from a wider range of subjects, within limits prescribed by the Secretary of State.

186.   Subsection (1) of section 65 replaces the whole section. It provides for the setting up of Academies. The basic model is the same as that for CTCs and city academies without some of the restrictions which apply to those schools.

- Academies can be set up anywhere in England (but not Wales). Unlike CTCs, CCTAs and city academies they are not limited to urban areas;

- Academies can, with the agreement of the Secretary of State, have an emphasis on any subject area, or combination of areas;

- Academies will be able to provide primary and/or secondary education, not just secondary education.

187.   Since the power to create CTCs, CCTAs and city academies is being

replaced, no more such schools will be created (but see sections 63 and 64 for what happens to existing schools).

188.   Subsection (2) of section 65 amends section 483 of the EA 96. It provides that the funding agreement for an Academy may make provision for the repayment of capital grants to the Secretary of State in the event of the termination of the funding agreement. This differs from the existing – and continuing – provisions for CTCs and CCTAs where the funding agreement must make provision for the repayment of capital grant to the Secretary of State in such an event.

189.   Subsection (3) of section 65 provides for a new Schedule (Schedule 7) which inserts a new Schedule (Schedule 35A) into the EA 96. This Schedule makes provision about land in relation to Academies. It largely repeats the provision that was made by Schedule 8 to the LSA for city academies.

190.   Part 2 of the Schedule amends existing legislation so as to put Academies in the same position as CTCs, CCTAs and city academies. Since, as explained below, existing city academies are to become Academies, this is chiefly a question of replacing references to city academies with references to Academies.

191.   The new Schedule also adds the following provisions:

- disapplication of the rule against perpetuities in relation to options granted in favour of an LEA where that land was transferred from that LEA to an Academy for no consideration. Without this disapplication the common law rule against perpetuities would limit to 21 years any option granted to return land to the LEA where the Academy closed or ceased to use the land;

- disapplication of section 153 of the Law of Property Act 1925 so that leaseholds of not less than 300 years granted by LEAs when transferring land for Academies cannot be enlarged into freeholds;

- an enabling provision for the Secretary of State to give class consent to allow LEAs to dispose of certain categories of land which had been used for the purposes of a county or community school.

Section 66: Arrangements for the admission of pupils to Academies

192.   This section amends section 85 of the SSFA by inserting section 85B, which may require, through regulations, an Admission Forum to advise Academies about local admission arrangements. Where such advice is promulgated, this section imposes a duty on the governing body of an

Academy to have regard to such advice.

Section 67: Conversion of city academies into Academies

193.   To avoid unnecessary multiplication of categories, section 67 provides that all existing city academies are technically to become 'Academies'. Their funding agreements are deemed to be made under the new provision (but are otherwise unchanged).

Section 68: City colleges

194.   In the case of an existing CTC or CCTA, a school may choose to change its name so that it becomes an Academy. In that case, its agreement will be deemed to be made under the new section 482. Otherwise CTCs and CCTAs are not affected by the new provisions.

Section 69: Uniform statutory trusts

195.   Section 69 provides for Academies and CTCs and CCTAs which provide denominational education to be added to denominational aided and foundation schools as the categories of schools which can benefit from funds held under uniform statutory trusts. Uniform statutory trusts are a standard type of statutory trust which may be incorporated in an order made by the Secretary of State in respect of a closed Church school, to allow the relevant Diocese to apply the proceeds of sale for the benefit of other Church schools.

Proposals to establish, alter or discontinue schools
Sections 70 to 75

Section 70 and Schedule 8: Proposals for additional secondary schools

196.   This section provides that LEAs in England may invite other people to make proposals for the establishment of a new community, foundation or voluntary secondary school or Academy that is not replacing such a school (an Academy is defined in section 65). Only after it has invited such proposals may it make proposals itself. At present proposals by an LEA to establish a new community or foundation secondary school are published under section 28 of the SSFA and decided through the arrangements for local decision making set out in that Act. The point of the change is to encourage a wider range of promoters to bring forward proposals to meet the need for a new school.

197.   The LEA must then:

- publish a notice inviting proposals for the establishment of an additional community, foundation or voluntary secondary school or Academy, and identifying a possible site for the school;

- publish any proposals that have been submitted in response to the notice;

- publish any proposals of its own that it wishes to make.

198. An LEA may not make proposals under section 28 of the SSFA when it could issue a notice under the new provision (see the amendment made by paragraph 94 of schedule 21).

199. Schedule 8 gives further details of the procedures to be followed and provides for regulations to further specify the necessary actions. In particular it provides for regulations to make provisions concerning comments by interested parties on the proposals that have been published.

200. Regulations will provide that following consultation the local SOC will be required to comment on the various options and to pass these comments to the Secretary of State who will then decide the proposals (or, in the case of an Academy, decide whether to enter into negotiations with the promoters with a view to signing a funding agreement with the Academy).

201. Proposals, which have been approved by the Secretary of State, are in general required to be implemented by the LEA which published the notice. However, a proposal for a voluntary controlled or foundation school may specify that the provision of the site will be the responsibility of the persons who made the proposal, and where a voluntary aided school is to be established at a site other than that specified in the notice, provision of the site will be the responsibility of the promoters.

202. If the land on which an Academy is to be sited is that identified in the notice published by the LEA, and certain other requirements are met, the Secretary of State may make a scheme for the transfer of the land to the promoters.

Section 71: Duty of LEAs to secure proposals

203. Where the Secretary of State is of the opinion that the provision for primary or secondary education in an area is, or is likely to become, insufficient, she may give a direction to the LEA to exercise its powers with a view to securing that provision is made for such additional number of pupils as is specified in the direction.

204. The LEA may use any combination of its existing powers to publish proposals under sections 28, 29 or 31 of the SSFA and the new powers of section 70 to invite proposals for the establishment of an additional community, foundation or voluntary secondary school or Academy. In meeting the direction the LEA must apply such principles as

are specified in the direction.

205.   The Secretary of State may also publish her own proposals for changes to schools or the establishment of new community or foundation schools to secure these places if the LEA does not comply with the direction within the time specified or she is not satisfied that the action taken by the LEA will secure the specified number of places. Regulations will prescribe the information to be contained in any proposals by the Secretary of State.

206.   Any such proposals will be decided by the local SOC or Schools Adjudicator under the existing provisions of Schedule 7 to the SSFA. That Schedule sets out the procedures that currently apply to proposals made by the Secretary of State to address an insufficiency or excess of school places.

Section 72 and Schedule 9: Proposals relating to sixth forms

207.   This section amends the LSA to enable the LSC in England, and the National Council for Education and Training for Wales (NCETW) to propose the establishment, alteration or closure of maintained school sixth forms. In exercising this power, the LSC is placed under an obligation to take account of any guidance from the Secretary of State. NCETW has an equivalent obligation in respect of guidance from the NAW. The section also provides for LSC proposals to be submitted to the Secretary of State, and for NCETW proposals to be submitted to the NAW, for decision; and for both the Secretary of State and the NAW to make regulations, as appropriate, setting out the processes, including the extent and nature of local consultation, to be followed by the LSC and NCETW in developing and submitting such proposals, and by the Secretary of State and the NAW in making a decision. The Schedule also specifies where responsibility lies for implementation of any approved proposals.

208.   Paragraph 115 of Schedule 21 amends Schedule 6 to the SSFA to enable regulations to be made which have the effect of providing that the SOC may not approve, and to provide that the LEA may not determine to implement, statutory proposals for changes to schools if they relate to undecided proposals by the LSC for the restructuring of sixth form education.

Section 73: Proposals by governing bodies of community schools

209.   This section amends section 28 of the SSFA to provide that in addition to the existing powers of the governing bodies of foundation and voluntary schools to publish proposals for prescribed alterations to schools, the governing bodies of community schools maintained by an LEA in England may also publish such proposals. It is intended that regulations will prescribe that community schools may make proposals to enlarge the premises of the school, to increase by 27 or more pupils the number in a

relevant age group to be admitted to the school, and to add a sixth form or extend a one-year sixth form to two years. At the moment only the LEA may publish such proposals in respect of community schools.

Section 74: Proposals for establishment of federated school

210.   This section makes provision for a new school to be established as a federated school under a single governing body from its opening date. It ensures that such schools should be subject to the existing arrangements governing statutory proposals set out in Chapter 2 of the SSFA to establish new community, voluntary or foundation special schools.

Section 75 and Schedule 10: Changes to existing procedures

211.   These provisions amend the procedure for dealing with statutory proposals for the establishment, alteration or discontinuance of schools in England. Schedule 6 to the SSFA 1998 is amended in relation to England to:

- allow comments of any kind, and not just objections, to be made in response to consultations in addition to statutory objections;

- allow the local SOC to refer statutory proposals to the Schools Adjudicator for decision if they think it appropriate to do so, subject to regulations (for example, if a Committee is unable to decide a proposal because it has not been possible to achieve a quorum. This may occur if many members of a Committee have an interest in the result of a matter that is being decided and they withdraw from the discussion of the matter);

- provide that promoters of new foundation or voluntary schools (other than Church of England or Roman Catholic dioceses, who already have groups on the SOC) whose proposals are rejected by the SOC shall have the right of appeal to the Adjudicator;

- provide that the governing bodies of foundation and voluntary schools of a prescribed description who have published proposals of a prescribed description shall have the right of appeal to the Adjudicator if their proposals are rejected by the SOC (the intention is to apply this to popular schools which have published proposals to expand);

- allow the LEA to refer proposals to the SOC for decision if it thinks it appropriate to do so and subject to regulations (this is intended to cover the situation where the proposals can only be approved conditionally, and therefore need to go to the SOC, since an LEA cannot make conditional approvals);

- provide that proposals approved conditionally by the SOC or Adjudicator shall no longer be treated as rejected if the condition is not met by the specified date, but instead shall be considered afresh by whoever gave the conditional approval.

212.   Schedule 6 to the SSFA is amended in relation to Wales to:

- Provide that proposals approved conditionally by the NAW shall no longer be treated as rejected if the condition is not met by the specified date, but instead shall be considered afresh.

213.   Schedule 7 to the SSFA, dealing with the Secretary of State's powers to act in the case of an insufficiency or excess of school places in an area, is also amended as necessary in the same way.

214.   Schedule 7 to the LSA, dealing with procedures for inadequate sixth forms, is also amended to the same effect.

PART 6 – THE CURRICULUM IN ENGLAND

Preliminary
Sections 76 and 77

215.   This Part re-enacts sections 350 to 368 of the EA 96 in their application to England, and thereby makes separate provision for a National Curriculum for England.

Section 76: Interpretation of Part 6

216.   This lists the definitions of terms used later in the Chapter.   They are mainly taken from the EA 96 except for:

- 'Foundation stage', which was a new stage introduced on a non-statutory basis in September 2000. It covers the period from age three to the end of the reception year in primary school. The foundation stage is organised in six areas of learning with early learning goals, which set out what most children are expected to achieve by the end of the foundation stage. The foundation stage is defined as a stage of the National Curriculum, but not as a key stage.

- 'Maintained nursery school', which is a school maintained by the LEA used mainly or wholly for the purpose of providing education for children who have attained the age of two but are under compulsory school age. It does not include a special school.

- 'Programmes of study', where the definition has been changed to mean the skills and processes which are required to be taught to pupils by the end of a key stage rather than during a key stage. This removes an implicit barrier in the legislation that pupils should only be taught material from the programme of study for their chronological age, making it clearer that teachers can allow pupils to proceed at a faster pace. Programmes of study are defined only in relation to key stages not the foundation stage.

Section 77: Meaning of 'nursery education' and related expressions

217. The inclusion of the foundation stage broadens the definition of the National Curriculum to include children below compulsory school age.

218. This section defines "nursery education" as education suitable for children below compulsory school age and defines "funded nursery education" as that provided by maintained schools, maintained nursery schools or by other providers who are receiving public funding to provide early years education.

General duties in respect of the curriculum
Sections 78 to 80

Sections 78 and 79: General requirements in relation to curriculum and duty to implement general requirements

219. These sections re-enact section 351 of the EA 96 with minor amendments.

Section 80: Basic curriculum for every maintained school in England

220. This section re-enacts section 352 of the EA 96, listing those elements (currently RE and sex education for certain pupils), which must be provided as part of the basic curriculum in addition to the National Curriculum.

221. The section provides for the inclusion of the foundation stage in the National Curriculum. This is done by changing the description of when the National Curriculum applies, so that it applies to children who have attained the age of three but are not over compulsory school age.

222. There is a new order-making power to alter the reference to compulsory school age (currently 16) so this could be amended to make some elements of curriculum provision statutory beyond 16.

223. There is also a new order making power for the Secretary of State to add to the list of further requirements, otherwise than in relation to RE or sex education. The power allows a new way to vary the curriculum requirements without affecting the National Curriculum, which has a distinct framework of key stages, attainment targets, programmes of study and assessment arrangements. This would enable new statutory

requirements for 14-16 year olds to be introduced, such as community activities.

The National Curriculum for England
Sections 81 to 89

Section 81 and 82: The foundation stage; The key stages

224.   These sections re-enact section 355 of the EA 96 and add the foundation stage to the National Curriculum. They set out the key stages in relation to a pupil, which are defined according to age. For example, key stage 2 begins when the majority of children in a pupil's class reach eight and ends when the majority of pupils in a class reach eleven.

225.   The foundation stage is defined as beginning when a child first receives publicly funded education on or after his or her third birthday and ending at the same time as the school year in which the child attains the age of five. Key stage 1 begins at the same time as the school year in which the child attains the age of six.

Section 83: Curriculum requirements for the foundation stage

226.   This section sets out the proposed content and structure of the foundation stage of the National Curriculum.

227.   The foundation stage comprises: early learning goals, which set out what most children are expected to achieve by the end of the foundation stage; six areas of learning; *Curriculum guidance for the foundation stage,* on which the education programmes of all publicly funded provision must be based; and a foundation stage profile, which assesses attainment at the end of the foundation stage. The foundation stage profile will summarise each child's progress in each area of learning and will provide substantial evaluative information about each child.

228.   The section also gives the Secretary of State power to amend the areas of learning.

Sections 84 to 86: The key stages in England and the power to alter or remove requirements for the fourth key stage

229.   Sections 84 and 85 re-enact sections 353 and 354 of the EA 96, listing the subjects which are compulsory at each key stage and stating that the National Curriculum is to specify attainment targets, programmes of study and assessment arrangements in relation to each subject for each key stage. Section 86 adds a broad power to alter or remove requirements for the fourth key stage.

230.   The requirements of the National Curriculum are now described separately in relation to the Foundation stage, key stages 1 to 3 and key

stage 4. This will allow for different provisions to apply at each stage. Separating out key stage 4 from the others allows for new requirements for this age group to be introduced in the future.

231.   In reproducing in sections 84 and 85 the lists of foundation subjects from section 354 of the EA 96, the reference to "technology" has been replaced by references to "design and technology" and "information and communication technology" (which are the subjects actually taught).

Section 87: Establishment of the National Curriculum for England by order

232.   This re-enacts section 356 of the EA 96 to include the foundation stage. The Secretary of State has order-making powers to specify in relation to each of the foundation stage areas of learning, early learning goals, educational programmes and assessment arrangements as appropriate; and in relation to the key stages the attainment targets, programmes of study and assessment arrangements which she considers appropriate for each subject. The previous prohibition on the subject of science including sexually transmitted diseases and human sexual behaviour has not been re-enacted.

233.   It extends order making powers in relation to the foundation stage to include all providers who are currently receiving Government early years education funding.

Section 88: Implementation of the National Curriculum for England in schools

234.   This re-enacts section 357 of the EA 96 in its application to England. It places a duty on LEAs, governing bodies and head teachers to ensure that the National Curriculum is implemented in maintained schools. This includes a new duty in respect of primary schools as the National Curriculum now includes the foundation stage.

Section 89: Implementation in respect of nursery schools etc

235.   This extends the duty to ensure that the foundation stage of the National Curriculum is implemented to include all providers who are receiving Government early years education funding.

The National Curriculum for England: special cases
Sections 90 to 95

Sections 90 to 95

236.   These sections re-enact sections 362-367 of the EA 96 for England, but add maintained nursery schools within the legislation.

Supplementary provisions
Section 96

Section 96: Procedure for making certain orders and regulations

237.   This section re-enacts section 368 of the EA 96 in its application to England.   It sets out the procedures which must be followed when the Secretary of State proposes to make orders or regulations relating to certain National Curriculum provisions.   She must refer her proposal to QCA, which will carry out a consultation on it and report back to the Secretary of State with the results of the consultation and their advice on it.   QCA's report must be published, as must the Secretary of State's response.   The Secretary of State must then publish and consult on a draft of the proposed order or regulations and a statement explaining her reasons if she is failing to give effect to any of QCA's recommendations.   After that consultation period has closed, she may make the order or regulations with or without modifications.

PART 7 – THE CURRICULUM IN WALES

Preliminary
Sections 97 and 98

238.   This Part re-enacts sections 350 to 368 of the EA 96 in their application to Wales, together with section 369 of that Act (which relates only to Wales). It thereby makes provision for a separate National Curriculum for Wales.

Sections 97 and 98: Interpretation of Part; meaning of "nursery education" and related expressions

239.   These sections are similar to sections 76 and 77 except that they apply to Wales.

General duties in respect of the curriculum
Sections 99 to 101

Sections 99 and 100: General requirements in relation to the curriculum and duty to implement general requirements

240.   These sections re-enact section 351 of the EA 96 except that section 100 requires LEAs and governing bodies to have regard to the NAW's guidance in exercising any functions in relation to any forms of education added to the basic curriculum by an order under section 101.

Section 101: Basic curriculum for every maintained school in Wales

241.   This section re-enacts section 352 of the EA 96, listing those elements (currently RE and sex education for certain pupils), which must be provided as part of the basic curriculum in addition to the National Curriculum for Wales.

242.   There is a new order making power for the NAW to add to the list further requirements, otherwise than in relation to RE or sex education. This new power also enables the NAW subsequently to amend or repeal anything that is added to the list of further requirements (apart from RE or sex education). The power allows a more flexible way to change statutory requirements than via the National Curriculum for Wales, which has a distinct framework of key stages, attainment targets, programmes of study and assessment arrangements. This would enable new statutory requirements for 14-16 year olds to be introduced. These would be different in nature from the academic subjects which now make up the National Curriculum for Wales.

The National Curriculum for Wales
Sections 102 to 110

Sections 102 and 103: The foundation stage; The key stages in Wales
243.   These sections re-enact section 355 of the EA 96. They set out the key stages in relation to a pupil, which are defined according to age. For example key stage 2 begins when the majority of children in a pupil's class reach eight and ends when the majority of pupils in a class reach eleven. They also provide for the period of the new foundation stage of the National Curriculum for Wales to be set out in an order of the NAW.

Section 104: Curriculum requirements for the foundation stage
244.   This is a new provision which provides that the foundation stage of the National Curriculum for Wales shall comprise areas of learning and, in respect of those areas, desirable outcomes, educational programmes and assessment arrangements. These are specified in an order made by the NAW under section 108(2).

Sections 105 to 107: The key stages in Wales and the power to alter or remove requirements for the fourth key stage
245.   Sections 105 and 106 re-enact sections 353 and 354 of the EA 96, listing the subjects which are compulsory at each key stage, but in relation to key stages 1, 2 and 3 only and stating that the National Curriculum shall specify attainment targets, programmes of study and assessment arrangements in relation to each subject for each key stage. Section 107 adds a broad power to alter or remove requirements for the fourth key stage.

246.   The requirements of the National Curriculum are now described separately in relation to the foundation stage, key stages 1 to 3 and key stage 4. This will allow for different provisions to apply at each stage. Separating out key stage 4 from the others allows for new requirements for this age group to be introduced in the future.

Section 108: Establishment of the National Curriculum for Wales by order

247.   This largely re-enacts section 356 of the EA 96 for key stage 4. It requires the NAW, by order, to specify areas of learning in respect of the foundation stage of the National Curriculum for Wales, and (in relation to each of those areas of learning) desirable outcomes, educational programmes and assessment arrangements.   Similarly it has power in relation to the 4 key stages to specify the attainment targets, programmes of study and assessment arrangements which it considers appropriate for each subject.

Section 109: Implementation of the National Curriculum for Wales in schools
248.   This re-enacts section 357 of the EA 96 in relation to Wales. It places a duty on LEAs, governing bodies and head teachers to ensure that the National Curriculum for Wales is implemented in maintained schools. This includes a new duty in respect of primary schools with nursery pupils in respect of the foundation stage.

Section 110: Implementation in respect of nursery schools etc.
249.   This extends the duty to ensure that the foundation stage of the National Curriculum is implemented to include head teachers, LEAs, and all providers who are currently receiving Government early years education funding.

The National Curriculum for Wales: special cases
Sections 111 to 116

Sections 111 to 116
250.   These sections re-enact sections 362-367 of the EA 96 for Wales.

Supplementary provisions
Sections 117 and 118

Section 117: Procedure for making certain orders and regulations
251.   This section requires the NAW to make such arrangements as it considers appropriate for consultation about proposals to make an order under section 103(4), 105(6), 108(2)(a) or (b)(i) or (ii) or (3)(a) or (b); or regulations under section 112.

Section 118: Programmes of research etc in relation to Wales
252.   This section re-enacts section 369 of the EA 96 for Wales, which enables the NAW to fund research and development relating to its National Curriculum functions.

PART 8 – TEACHERS

Teachers' Pay and Conditions

Sections 119 to 130

Section 119 & Schedule 11: School Teachers' Review Body

253.   This section affirms the continued existence of the School Teachers' Review Body (STRB) set up under the STPCA. The arrangements will continue to apply to England and Wales. The section also provides that the members of the STRB will be appointed by the Secretary of State, rather than by the Prime Minister as under the STPCA. This will bring the appointment of members of the STRB into line with similar bodies, reflecting the general move away from Prime Ministerial appointments. The Chairman of the STRB will, however, continue to be appointed by the Prime Minister. Schedule 11 reflects consequential changes. The Schedule recasts Schedule 1 to the STPCA and makes minor simplifications and modifications to it. Matters covered are STRB membership, arrangements for the appointment of a chairman and deputy chairman, resignation and dismissal arrangements, payments to members and proceedings of the STRB.

Section 120: Review Body: function

254.   Under this section, the STRB will, as at present, report on school teachers' remuneration and related conditions of employment (professional duties and working time), at the request and under the direction of the Secretary of State, including on the timing of a report. Any such report will be sent to the Prime Minister and the Secretary of State and published.

Section 121: Consultation by Review Body

255.   This section requires bodies which the STRB deems it appropriate to consult to be notified of any referral to them by the Secretary of State. The 'relevant bodies' for consultation are LEA associations, LEAs, organisations representing governors of maintained schools, and bodies representing school teachers (teacher unions). These bodies must be given an opportunity to submit evidence and make representations. The STRB will be explicitly able to determine the way in which the relevant bodies are entitled to respond and may limit this as appropriate. For example, if the STRB considered it appropriate, some bodies could be permitted to respond in writing only.

256.   The section also gives the Secretary of State a formal entitlement to submit evidence and make representations. This has been accepted practice hitherto.

Section 122: Power to prescribe pay and conditions

257.   This section enables the Secretary of State to make orders determining school teachers' pay, working time and professional duties. This replicates the existing structure whereby such orders legally define school teachers' conditions of employment by reference to a document. As

at present, school teachers must be paid only in accordance with such orders and nothing in a teacher's contract which is prohibited by or inconsistent with an order will be effective.

258.   The section also defines 'school teacher'. A school teacher provides primary or secondary education under a contract of employment or a contract for services, where the other party to the contract is the governing body of a maintained school or an LEA. This includes teachers who are self-employed, but excludes those who are employed by an agency such as a teacher supply agency. A school teacher will either be a qualified teacher, as defined elsewhere under regulation; or unqualified, as prescribed by order.   The latter category will encompass overseas-trained teachers, instructors, and those following the Graduate or Registered Teacher Programme routes. The definition also specifically includes anyone serving as a head teacher of a school maintained by a local education authority, which will ensure that all relevant head teachers are covered by pay and conditions orders made under this section. Teachers employed by local authorities for social services purposes are excluded from the definition.

Section 123: Order under section 122: scope

259.   This section sets out some specific matters which the orders under the previous section may cover. It is not an exhaustive list. An order may confer discretions on LEAs or governing bodies. It may also confer a function on the Secretary of State or on another person who has agreed to carry it out. This may cover matters such as assessments or the exercise of a discretion. In practice this would include arrangements such as those relating to threshold or fast track assessment. An order may also require that any guidance issued relating to such matters is taken into account. Appeals rights may also be set out in an order.

260.   Orders may also enable a teacher's pay to be set with regard to qualifications, experiences, duties, skills or previous salary, though this does not exclude other factors from being taken into account.   The reference to previous salary is to make clear that there are, for example, powers to safeguard teachers' previous teaching salary in certain specific cases where they have moved to other posts, such as where there are statutory school closures or reorganisations. Limits on payments may be set and certain provisions may be applied to certain schools. For example, there are at present special arrangements for calculating the pay of head teachers of special schools.

261.   Retrospective provision is allowed by order under this section, but not so as to reduce a teacher's remuneration, or alter a teacher's conditions of employment to his or her disadvantage, prior to the order. Orders may also specify that certain matters are not to be treated as remuneration, or related to professional duties or working time. This will enable it to be

made clear that certain conditions of employment should be determined locally.

Section 124: Order under section 122: supplemental

262.   This section provides for an order made under section 122 to make provision through a document, which must also be published. This means that current practice, whereby a document which sets out all appropriate pay and conditions requirements is brought into effect by a pay order, can continue.

Section 125: Reference to Review Body

263.   This section sets out the circumstances in which the Secretary of State may make an order under section 122. Usually, as at present, the provision in an order will follow a request for a report to the STRB, and the STRB's response. But the section also makes some changes to the Secretary of State's powers. At present, the STPCA allows the Secretary of State to make orders relating to matters which she does not consider so significant as to require referral to the STRB. The section here enables the Secretary of State to make an order where the matter concerned is subsidiary; or where the STRB's chairman is consulted on disapplying the provision requiring detailed consideration by the STRB.

264.   The section explains what 'subsidiary' means for this purpose. It will cover the standards which the Secretary of State may set for different classes of teachers – for example, Advanced Skills Teachers – and criteria for progression from one pay scale to another – this would cover movement from the main pay scale to the upper pay scale following threshold assessment. (It should be noted that this does not mean that the Secretary of State will take decisions without involving the STRB on whether such categories of teachers or such pay scales should exist at all.)

265.   Minor but necessary amendments could in future also be made to pay orders without reference back to the STRB in order to cover issues arising from the implementation of their recommendations, for example to ensure that groups of teachers are not disadvantaged, or to make recommendations work in practice. This might cover matters such as the complex arrangements necessary for the payment of recruitment and retention allowances, and assimilation arrangements resulting from changes to the pay structure. The matters might also be those which are minor in policy effect and therefore do not need to be subject to the full rigour of the STRB process, such as a desirable adjustment following on from a main policy or an interpretation of the intention, for example a change in the way training days are calculated to enable teachers to be paid for additional training undertaken in the evenings.

266.   The section also gives the Secretary of State power by order to

determine that provision of a particular kind should be, or cease to be, subsidiary, and to describe this provision by reference to her own opinion or to the opinion of another person. Section 210 provides for an order making such a determination to be subject to affirmative resolution procedure.

Section 126: Consultation by the Secretary of State

267.   This section requires the Secretary of State to consult appropriate bodies before making any order under section 122 or section 125(4)(a). The relevant bodies are again LEAs and LEA associations, governor bodies, and bodies representing school teachers (teacher unions). Consultation with relevant bodies takes place under existing arrangements for making pay orders and is an important part of the review process. The consultation requirement relating to section 125(4)(a) relates to the Secretary of State's power to make an order identifying a certain provision as 'subsidiary', which may be used where such a provision is not already covered in section 125(3).

Section 127: Guidance

268.   This section enables the Secretary of State to issue guidance on how any order made under section 122 should be put into practice, and requires LEAs and governing bodies to have regard to it.   There must be consultation with the usual parties (as above) before any guidance may be issued. LEAs and governing bodies are expected to follow such guidance, and this section provides that a court or tribunal could take failure to do so into account in any proceedings.

Section 128: Education action zone

269.   As at present under section 3 of the STPCA, this section entitles the governing body of a school in an EAZ to seek permission from the Secretary of State for it to determine the pay and conditions of the teachers at its school. This must, as at present, follow consultation with all the teachers at its school. The section provides a new power for the Secretary of State to make regulations to deal with the situation which could arise if the opt out should end for a particular reason.

Section 129: Transfer of employment

270.   This section carries forward the current arrangements about Transfer of Undertakings and provides that pay and conditions orders shall not apply to any teacher of a previously independent school which becomes a maintained school, including a maintained nursery school, except at the request of the teacher.

Section 130: Repeal

271.   This section repeals the STPCA. As described above, most of the STPCA is being re-enacted in the new legislation, with minor modifications

where necessary.

School Teachers' Appraisal
Section 131

Section 131: Appraisal

272.   This section updates existing powers under section 49 of the Education (No. 2) Act 1986 (EA 86) under which the Secretary of State, or the NAW, may make regulations requiring appraisal of the performance of schoolteachers employed under national pay and conditions and teachers in FE. Further, this section makes explicit: that the regulations can impose duties on specified groups of people in relation to the appraisal of teachers' performance; that the appraisal process may involve the exercise of a discretion conferred on persons identified in the regulations, for example, head teachers, governors and those teachers appointed by the headteacher to review performance; and that schools may use appraisal data in pay decisions. Before making regulations under this section the Secretary of State will consult bodies which she thinks appropriate. This section repeals section 49 of the EA 86.

School Teachers' qualifications
Sections 132 to 135

Section 132: Qualified teacher status

273.   This section and section 133 re-enact and amend section 218 (1)(a) and (2) of the Education Reform Act 1988 (ERA) by defining the term 'qualified teacher'. It provides that the Secretary of State continues to have the power to determine who is a qualified teacher.

Section 133: Requirement to be qualified

274.   This is a new regulatory power. Under the provisions of this section, the Secretary of State may set out the specified work which only qualified teachers may carry out in schools. In addition, certain other persons may carry out this work in schools if they satisfy specified requirements. The unqualified teachers who are permitted to be employed in schools under the current secondary legislation will continue to do so and they will be able to carry out the specified work in the same circumstances as previously. The section will also provide for teaching assistants and teaching support staff to carry out the specified work in schools if they are appropriately supervised.

Section 134: Requirement to be registered

275.   Under this section, the Secretary of State, or the NAW, may by regulations provide that a specified activity may be carried out in a school maintained by an LEA or a non-maintained special school by a qualified teacher only where that teacher is registered with full registration with the

General Teaching Council (GTC) for England or for Wales. It also provides that a trainee teacher may undertake a specified course of training leading to qualified teacher status only where that teacher is registered with provisional registration with the GTC for England or for Wales. In addition provisional registration may be required of unqualified teachers undertaking specified work in schools.

Section 135: Head teachers

276.   This section provides that the Secretary of State and the NAW may by regulations make it compulsory for persons serving as head teachers to be qualified teachers. Also the Secretary of State and the NAW may by regulations make it compulsory for first-time head teachers to hold a specified qualification if they are appointed on or after the date when the regulations come into force. Subsection (5) makes clear that the Regulations will apply to LEA-maintained schools and non-maintained special schools.

Further education
Sections 136 to 140

Section 136: Provision of education

277.   This section enables the Secretary of State to make regulations which have the effect of requiring FE teachers to have a specified qualification and which can require lecturers to serve a probationary period. This section re-enacts section 218(1)(a), (c) and (d) of the ERA with amendments.

Section 137: Principals of further education institutions

278.   This section provides that the Secretary of State may make regulations making it compulsory for the principal of an FE college to have a specified qualification, which could include an induction programme. The regulations may allow a person to serve as principal while he is undertaking the induction programme within a specified period of time.

Section 138: Training in provision of further education

279.   This section enables the Secretary of State to make regulations regulating the provision of courses which lead to a teaching qualification for an FE teacher or an FE principal qualification under sections 136 and 137. This section makes provision similar to that in section 218(9)(b) and (c) of the ERA.

Section 139: Wales: provision of higher education

280.   This section allows the NAW to make regulations relating to the provision of courses of higher education at FE institutions in Wales. The section re-enacts section 218(9)(d) of the ERA so as to enable regulations to prohibit provision of such courses without the NAW's approval and to

regulate the numbers and categories of students on such courses. This provision will assist the NAW to assist in the planning of post 16 learning provision in Wales.

Section 140: Further education: general

281.   This section permits exceptions to the regulations created under sections 136 to 139 and identifies the bodies that may have a function imposed on them under those sections. It also includes a definition of "education" which applies to sections 136-139. This definition includes certain types of training and reflects part of the definition of "further education" in the EA 96.

Health and fitness
Section 141

Section 141: Health and fitness

282.   This section re-enacts section 218(5) of the ERA with a minor amendment. The Secretary of State and the NAW continue to have power to impose requirements as to the health and physical capacity of persons such as teachers in schools and further education institutions. In addition the Secretary of State and the NAW may impose requirements as to the health and physical capacity of persons who are employed by LEAs or governing bodies otherwise than as teachers and who are regularly in contact with persons aged under 18. Section 218(5) of the ERA refers to persons aged under 19.

Misconduct etc.
Sections 142 to 144

Section 142: Prohibition from teaching etc.

283.   This section re-enacts and modifies the Secretary of State's power in section 218(6) of the ERA to prohibit or restrict the employment of teachers and workers with children. The Secretary of State and, in Wales, the Secretary of State and the NAW acting concurrently continue to have power to make directions prohibiting a person from: providing education at a school, FE institution or LEA; taking part in the management of an independent school; or carrying out work, in relation to schools, FE institutions or LEAs, that brings the person regularly into contact with children aged under 18 years (the current provision refers to persons aged under 19). The section provides the Secretary of State and the NAW with the power to prevent a person from working for a company exercising functions on behalf of a local education authority, a person working for a contractor and a person working voluntarily.

284.   The Secretary of State and the NAW can prohibit or restrict someone's employment on the grounds of his misconduct, that he is

unsuitable to work with children, that he is included permanently on the list of people considered unsuitable to work with children that is kept by the Secretary of State for Health under the Protection of Children Act 1999 (POCA), or on medical grounds. The Secretary of State and the NAW will also have power to direct that a person may not take part in the management of an independent school on grounds of that person's professional incompetence. The power to make directions on educational grounds is to be repealed. The Secretary of State and the NAW will have power to revoke or vary a direction except where a direction was given on the grounds that a person is unsuitable to work with children and that person claims he is no longer unsuitable. Provision is made for the procedure for making directions and the grounds on which a person may seek to have a direction revoked or varied to be set out in regulations. The section also provides for the enforcement of this duty.

Section 143: Directions under section 142: contractor, agency, etc

285. This section imposes a duty on bodies such as employment agencies or businesses, contractors, or voluntary organisations, that provide or employ individuals to do work that is within section 142 (2) or (3) not to arrange for an individual who is subject to a direction under section 142 to carry out any work that would contravene that direction. Such organisations will have to ensure that any person they propose to provide or employ to do such work is not subject to a direction that would prevent him or her from undertaking the work in question. If the Secretary of State or NAW think that such a body is likely to fail to comply with the duty they may issue a direction to secure compliance. Such a direction may require the body to take or refrain from taking steps specified in the direction. The direction may be enforced by the S/S or NAW by a mandatory order

Section 144: Directions under section 142: appeal

286. This section partially re-enacts section 218A of the ERA to allow a person who is subject to a direction under section 142 to appeal against a decision to make a direction or not to revoke or vary a direction. It provides for appeals to be heard by the Tribunal established under section 9 of the POCA. The section also allows a person who is subject to a direction on the grounds that he is unsuitable to work with children to apply to the Tribunal for a review of the direction. The Secretary of State or the NAW may make regulations preventing an appeal being made on the grounds that the person did not commit an offence of which he has been convicted. Regulations may also set out the circumstances in which the Tribunal will allow an appeal or grant an application for a review and the powers available to the Tribunal on allowing an appeal or granting a review.

Sections 132 to 140: general
Sections 145 and 146

Section 145: Specification of qualification

287.   Regulations made in relation to teachers' qualifications may refer to initial teacher training (ITT) courses at accredited institutions and may confer a discretion on the Teacher Training Agency or Higher Education Funding Council for Wales, or other specified persons or bodies. The regulations may also impose a duty on the Teacher Training Agency. The Secretary of State has to consult the GTC about changes to the content of initial teacher training.

Section 146: Repeal of sections 218 and 218A of the Education Reform Act 1988

288.   This section repeals sections 218 and 218A of the ERA.

1999 Pay document
Section 147

Section 147: Application of pay-scale

289.   School teachers' pay and conditions are determined under the provisions of the STPCA, and set out in the School Teachers' Pay and Conditions Document which is updated as of September each year. Until 31 August 1999, the school teachers' pay spine comprised 18 points, numbered 0 to 17. Two points were awarded for possession of a good honours degree, and points were awarded incrementally for years of experience up to a total of 9 points for both qualifications and experience. Points could also be awarded on the basis of other criteria. Newly qualified teachers normally started on point 0 or point 2, depending upon whether or not they were a good honours graduate.

290.   With effect from 1 September 1999, point 0 was removed and the differential for good honours degrees reduced to 1 point for new entrants. Subsequently, the Department formed the view that the legal effect of the amendments was uncertain. The Department sought to remedy this by means of a remedial order, which took effect on 1 April 2000. However the Department believes that the order did not resolve the matter fully. This section now seeks to tidy up the way in which point 0 was removed in order to ensure that all teachers' true lawful pay entitlement is clearly the entitlement intended in the 1999 and subsequent School Teachers' Pay and Conditions Documents. The provisions should work in practice by making no difference to teachers' pay.

General Teaching Councils for England and Wales
Section 148

Section 148 and Schedule 12: The General Teaching Councils

291.   This Schedule amends section 2 of the Teaching and Higher Education Act 1998 (THEA) by extending the existing advisory functions

of the GTCs for England and for Wales.

292.   The Schedule amends section 3 of the THEA (relating to the registration of teachers with the GTCs for England and for Wales) giving the Secretary of State or the NAW power to introduce a new category of provisional registration of teachers. Eligibility for such registration will be defined in the regulations, and is expected to apply to trainee teachers and overseas teachers. Registration for teachers with qualified teacher status is consequently redefined as "full" registration.

293.   The Schedule also provides that a person will not be eligible for registration, whether full or provisional, unless he or she has been judged by the GTCs as suitable to be a teacher. It will be for the GTCs to determine suitability. They might, for example, wish to satisfy themselves as to the good character of individuals by means of criminal record checks and character references for overseas teachers. Amendments to the Police Act 1997 provide that the GTCs have access to criminal records. The GTCs will exercise their functions on the assessment of suitability at the point that a person applies to become provisionally registered or re-registered; or fully registered or re-registered.

294.   The Schedule provides for a right of appeal to the High Court against a refusal of an application for registration on the grounds of suitability. The power to make regulations in section 4 of the THEA is extended so that an applicant so refused may be informed of the reasons for the decision and of his or her right of appeal.

295.   Section 4 of the THEA is also amended to provide that the GTCs, in setting the level of the fee, should have regard to expenditure on all their functions, including registration.

296.   The Schedule extends the functions of the GTCs to include activities designed to promote the standing of the teaching profession.

297.   The Schedule amends Schedule 1 to the THEA to allow the Secretary of State and the NAW by order to amend certain provisions of Schedule 1 with a view to removing or relaxing the controls which they exercise over the GTCs for England and Wales respectively – for example, to remove the need for their consent to the borrowing of money by the GTCs, or to the provision of pension schemes.

298.   The Schedule amends Schedule 2 to the THEA to allow the GTCs to attach conditions to any suspension order made in relation to a teacher against whom they bring disciplinary proceedings. Where a suspension order is made, the teacher's name is removed from the register. Under the amendment, the teacher would be required to comply with any conditions –

for example, to undertake a course of counselling – before he or she is eligible to be registered again.

299.   The Schedule also amends Schedule 2 to the THEA to provide that references to registration mean either full or provisional registration.

PART 9 – CHILDCARE AND NURSERY EDUCATION

Childcare
Sections 149 to 152

Sections 149 and 150: Duties of LEA in respect of childcare; Early years development partnerships and plans

300.   Early Years Development Partnerships were established by section 119 of the SSFA to plan and co-ordinate Early Years Education in each LEA area. In May 1998, on a non-statutory basis, Partnerships took on the additional role of planning and co-ordinating childcare and the newly formed Early Years Development and Childcare Partnerships (EYDCPs) commenced operation in April 1999.

301.   Section 149 inserts into the SSFA a new section 118A which places a duty on LEAs to carry out annual reviews of childcare provision in their area and establish and maintain an information service on childcare and other related services.

302.   Section 19 of the CA requires local authorities to review the provision of day care and childminding within their area. Section 149 now incorporates these requirements and therefore section 19 is to be repealed with respect to England and Wales only.

303.   The amendments made by section 150 confer duties relating to childcare on LEAs in addition to those set out in the SSFA with respect to Nursery Education. Section 150 (2) ensures that childcare will now be included in LEAs' Plans and together with 150 (1) and 150 (4) will ensure that the Plans take into account the review of childcare which LEAs are required to undertake in Section 149. As the Plans will now include childcare, section 150 (5) renames Early Years Development Partnerships (EYDPs) as Early Years Development and Childcare Partnerships (EYDCPs). This name is already in use by the LEA and the Partnerships. Section 150 (4) sets out the approval requirements by the Secretary of State or the NAW and the publication arrangements.

Section 151: Childcare functions of HMCI and National Assembly for Wales

304.   The Tax Credits Act 2002 includes provision which will enable

certain costs incurred on childcare to be taken into account in calculating an individual's entitlement to certain tax credits. That Act makes provision for the relevant childcare costs to be identified. The providers of the childcare will have to be approved in accordance with a scheme set out in the regulations.

305.   This section allows the Secretary of State, by order, to confer on HMCI whatever functions are necessary or expedient to allow HMCI to be able to operate a childcare scheme set out in regulations made under the Tax Credits Act 2002. Functions are conferred on HMCI by Part 10A of the CA with regard to regulation and inspection of childcare in England. These may not extend to all functions that may be needed to operate a childcare scheme. This provision enables additional functions to be conferred for that purpose.

306.   It also allows the NAW to have additional functions specified in an order made by the NAW which are necessary or expedient to allow the NAW to operate a childcare scheme under the Tax Credits Act 2002. Such an order may only specify functions corresponding to those conferred by the Secretary of State on HMCI under the preceding subsection.

Section 152 and Schedule 13: Regulation of child minding and day care

307.   Schedule 13 amends Part 10A of and Schedule 9A to the CA. Part 10A of the CA was inserted by section 79 of the Care Standards Act 2000 and transferred the function of regulating persons who act as child minders or who provide day care from local authorities to HMCI in England and the NAW in Wales. The amendments proposed include:

- **Consent to checks on suitability**: The registration authority (HMCI in England and the NAW in Wales) is required under the CA to determine whether a person is qualified for registration as a child minder or a provider of day care. A person is so qualified if he is suitable to look after children under the age of eight and if his "associates" are suitable to look after or (as the case may be) to be in regular contact with children under the age of eight. "Associates" in this context means persons who look after children on premises on which child minding or day care takes place, persons who live or are employed on the premises (in the case of child minding) or who live and work on the premises (in the case of day care). As part of this assessment of a person's suitability, the registration authority will need to carry out certain checks (eg criminal record checks) on individuals. This provision permits the registration authority to treat failure by a person or his associates to give consent to a check as a ground on which it may conclude that the person in question is not suitable and consequently that a person is not qualified for registration.

- **Suspension of registration**: An amendment to section 79H of the CA will ensure that a person whose registration is suspended under regulations made by virtue of that section, but who continues to operate as a childminder or day care provider, will, in the absence of reasonable excuse, be committing an offence in the same way as a person who acts as a childminder or provides day care without being registered.

- **Rights of appeal in relation to registration**: An amendment to section 79M of the CA permits the matters which may be brought before the tribunal established under section 9 of the POCA (the Care Standards Tribunal (CST)) to be extended. This provision gives the Secretary of State and the NAW the power to prescribe in regulations additional decisions arising under Part 10A which may be appealed to the CST. For example, decisions on the issue of certificates of suitability for persons working with children over the age of seven under section 79W of the CA cannot be appealed to the CST at present, but would be able to be included through regulations made under the proposed provision.

- **Inspections by HMCI**: An amendment to section 79Q of the CA allows the inspections to be carried out either by the Chief Inspector (ie Ofsted) directly as well as by registered inspectors (as allowed for in the powers of delegation available to the Chief Inspector in the SIA). The amendment is needed because many inspectors are now employees of Ofsted rather than independent contractors. This provision applies to England only.

- **Rights of entry**: An amendment to section 79U of the CA will ensure that an inspector is authorised by the registration authority before he or she has the right of entry. Existing legislation gives right of entry to inspectors by virtue of being registered alone.

- **Disqualification for registration**: An amendment to Schedule 9A of the CA will introduce a power for regulations to be made permitting the registration authority to waive disqualification for registration where a person has disclosed to the registration authority a matter (eg criminal conviction) which would under existing regulations lead to that person's disqualification. If the registration authority withdraws its consent to registration, a person will once more be disqualified. It is intended that the registration authority will give consent where it considers the reason for disqualification irrelevant to registration. This power was previously available to local authorities when they were responsible for registration and inspection.

- The Schedule also includes amendments to sections 113 and 115 of the Police Act 1997 which provide, respectively, for the issue of criminal record certificates and enhanced criminal record certificates. These amendments make three main changes to existing legislation.

- First, they ensure that when a criminal record certificate is applied for under section 113 as part of the registration authority's assessment of a person's suitability certain additional matters specific to a person's suitability to work with children (such as whether a person is included in the list kept under section 1 of the POCA) can be obtained not only in relation to persons applying to be registered, or already registered, but also in relation to their "associates" (as defined in the first bullet of this paragraph above). At present the legislation only permits this in relation to the former categories.

- Second, the amendments provide that the enhanced criminal record certificate (under section 115), as well as the criminal record certificate (under section 113), can contain the additional matters specific to a person's suitability to work with children, where such a certificate is applied for in connection with registration under Part 10A.

- Third, the amendments provide that a criminal record certificate and an enhanced criminal record certificate (including the additional matters referred to above) can be obtained in relation to an applicant for, or a holder of, a certificate under section 79W and his associates. Section 79W applies, broadly, to a person who looks after or provides care to children over the age of seven and under the age of 15 or, in the case of disabled children, 17.

Nursery Education
Sections 153 to 156

Section 153: Powers of LEA in respect of funded nursery education

308.   This section provides that where, in the exercise of the duty imposed on them by section 118 of SSFA to ensure provision of nursery education in their area, an LEA makes financial assistance available to nursery education providers in the non-maintained sector, they must take account of any guidance which may be issued by the Secretary of State, or in the case of Wales, the NAW.

309.   The guidance will be based on existing requirements that already

apply to payment of Nursery Education grant and will set out specific conditions and qualitative requirements that providers of nursery education must meet. It will enable LEAs to monitor the quality of provision and to control the terms upon which funding is paid to such providers. It will also help to ensure that the providers meet the conditions attached to the funding. If they fail to meet such conditions, then repayment of any financial assistance made to them by the LEA may be required.

Section 154: Establishment or alteration of maintained nursery schools

310.   This section amends section 28(1) of the SSFA to provide that if an LEA wishes to establish a maintained nursery school it must publish proposals to do so. LEAs must already publish proposals if they wish to close a nursery school or establish a community or foundation school.

311.   For Wales, the section also amends section 28 of the SSFA to require an LEA to publish proposals to make any prescribed alteration to a maintained nursery school. Alterations to be prescribed as requiring the publication of proposals are likely to include changes in the main language of instruction, relocation to a new site, and significant enlargement.

Section 155 and Schedule 14: Inspection of nursery education

312.   This section gives effect to Schedule 14 which amends Schedule 26 to the SSFA. The amendments cover the following:

- **Conduct of inspections by Inspectorate**: Nursery education is currently inspected by registered nursery inspectors, i.e. inspectors of nursery education placed on a register by HMCI in England or Her Majesty's Chief Inspector of Education and Training in Wales (each referred to here as the "Chief Inspector"). The conditions governing such an inspector's registration, removal from the register, appeal rights, etc. are contained in Schedule 26 to the SSFA. Ofsted intend that the majority of nursery education inspection work will, in future, be carried out by suitably qualified childcare inspectors who are Ofsted employees. It is not considered necessary for such employees, whose qualifications and activities are governed by their employment contract with Ofsted, to also be subject to the registration process currently described in Schedule 26 of the SSFA. The amendments make two main changes to the current regime.

- First, paragraph 1 of Schedule 14 makes an amendment to paragraph 6 of Schedule 26 of the SSFA which permits inspection to be carried either by registered nursery inspectors, as now, or by members of the inspectorate, which includes the Chief Inspector and his employees. This means that, for example, in relation to England, HMCI can use Ofsted employees (in particular, suitably qualified child care inspectors) to carry out such inspections without them having also to comply with provisions relating to registration which are inappropriate to an employee's status.

- Second, paragraph 2 of Schedule 14 makes an amendment to paragraph 8 of Schedule 26, which changes the regime applying to registered nursery inspectors in order to give the Chief Inspector more control over who is placed on the register. At present, anyone may apply for registration and has a right to have his application considered and then to be registered if he fulfils statutory criteria.

- **Appeals**: The Registered Nursery Inspector's Tribunal (RNIT) established by Schedule 26 to the SSFA, currently hears any appeal against the removal of a registered nursery inspector from the register, as well as a refusal to renew registration and any imposition or variation in conditions attaching to registration. Under Part 10A of the CA, the Tribunal established by section 9 of the POCA (the CST), when it is set up, will hear any appeal against the removal of early years child care inspectors from the register. This provision will enable registered nursery inspector appeals to be heard in England by the CST rather than the RNIT, giving a single point for appeals from early years child care inspectors and registered nursery inspectors against, among other matters, removal from the two registers.

Section 156: Meaning of "nursery school" and "primary education"

313.   This section amends the definitions of "nursery school" and "primary education" in the EA 96.

314.   Section 6 of the EA 96 states that a primary school is a nursery school if it is used mainly for the purpose of providing education for children who have attained the age of two but are under compulsory school age.   The purpose of the amendment is to clarify that this definition of "nursery school" includes schools which are used wholly for the provision of education for children between the ages of two and compulsory school age.

315.   The general definition of primary education currently refers to full-time education suitable to the requirements of junior pupils who have not attained the age of ten years and six months.   While this covers pupils below compulsory school age it does not reflect the common practice in nursery schools of offering education for either the morning or the afternoon session - nursery schools may offer education in both morning and afternoon sessions, but often to a different cohort of pupils.   Some pupils under compulsory school age do attend a school full-time, for instance in the reception class of a primary school.   A widening of the

definition to cover part-time nursery education will recognise the prevalence of part-time education at the nursery stage.

PART 10 – INDEPENDENT SCHOOLS

316.   This Part enacts a new statutory regime for independent schools to replace the existing regime in Part 7 of the EA 96.

Chapter 1 – Regulation of independent schools
Sections 157-171

Standards
Section 157

Section 157: Independent school standards
317.   This section confers power on the Secretary of State (or, in Wales, the NAW) to prescribe standards which independent schools must meet in order to be, or to remain, registered.

Requirement of registration
Sections 158 and 159

Section 158: The registers
318.   This section provides for the continuation of existing registers, kept by the Secretary of State and the NAW for England and Wales respectively.

Section 159: Unregistered schools
319.   The section makes it an offence to operate an independent school which is not registered, and establishes a new power to enable HMI to enter premises where there is reasonable cause to believe that an unregistered independent school is operating illegally.   The section specifies the penalties for conducting an unregistered school and obstructing HMI's right of entry.

Registration procedure
Sections 160 and 161

Sections 160 and 161: Applications for registration and Determination of applications for registration
320.   Section 160 sets out the information to be provided with an application for registration and provides for HMI to inspect. Section 161 ensures that independent schools meet prescribed standards before registration.

Enforcement of prescribed standards after registration

Sections 162 to 167

Section 162: Changes to registered details

321.   This section enables the registration authority to remove a school from the register when there has been a material change which has not been approved. It requires the proprietor of an independent school to notify the Secretary of State, or the NAW, of specified variations in the details of the school's registration so that the new provision can be approved, where appropriate, following an inspection.

Section 163: Power to inspect registered schools

322.   Subsection (1) makes provision for inspections by registered inspectors, HMI and any 'approved body'.   The Independent Schools Inspectorate (ISI) will be an 'approved body' for this purpose. In fact, the ISI already undertake inspections of independent schools in England in membership of associations affiliated to the Independent Schools Council. The section also requires reports to be made to the Secretary of State or the NAW for their publication.

Section 164: Inspections: supplementary

323.   This section deals with a range of supplementary inspection issues including at subsection (9) provision for the introduction of charges by Ofsted or Estyn (the education and training inspectorate for Wales) for inspections of registered schools.

Section 165: Failure to meet standards

324.   The section introduces a new regime for dealing with independent schools where standards are not being maintained. Subsection (2) refers specifically to a fast track arrangement when a school is failing to meet the required standards and there is a serious risk to pupils' welfare. In all other cases schools found not to be meeting the standards will be required to produce, and subsequently implement, an action plan to remedy the areas of concern.

Sections 166 and 167: Appeals and determination of appeals

325.   Where action is taken against a school failing to meet the standards under section 165, provision is made in 166 for an appeal to a standing tribunal (the CST). An order or determination made by the Secretary of State will not take effect until the school has had an opportunity to lodge an appeal. The tribunal will, however, have the power to make an order for interim suspension under subsection (5) of this section if it considers there is a risk of serious harm occurring to pupils pending the determination of the appeal. Section 167 sets out the powers of the tribunal.

Supplementary
Sections 168 to 171

Section 168: Provision of information

326.   This section reproduces the substance of the existing section 467 of the EA 96 regarding the provision of information about registered and provisionally registered schools but also creates a new offence of failing to provide the required information to be punishable by a fine.

Section 169: Unsuitable persons

327.   The section empowers the Secretary of State or the NAW to remove an independent school from the Register, if the proprietor or any other person employed at the school is acting in contravention of a direction or order which prohibits them from working with children.

Sections 170 to 171: Service of notice etc. and Interpretation of Chapter 1

328.   This section deals with the duties imposed on the Secretary of State or the NAW when giving notice of decisions, determinations or orders. Section 171 provides definitions for terms used in Chapter 1 of this Part.

Children with special educational needs
Sections 172 to 174

Section 172: Alteration to definition of "independent school"

329.   The section amends the EA 96 to define a school as an independent school if it provides full time education for five or more pupils of compulsory school age or if it has just one pupil with a statement of SEN or who is looked after by a public authority and it is not a maintained school or a special school not so maintained.

Section 173: Right of access of LEA

330.   Section 327 of the EA 96 provides that LEAs have access to certain schools to monitor provision made for children with SEN. This section adds independent schools to the list of establishments to which LEAs have a right of access.

Section 174: Consent to placement

331.   Section 347 (5)(b) of the EA 96 provides for the Secretary of State, or the NAW, to give consent to placement at an independent school which does not have approval as being suitable to provide special education. This section adds the condition that the Secretary of State, or the NAW, must be satisfied that there is a place available at the school before considering or granting consent to the placing authority. It will be for the Local Authority as placing authority to demonstrate that there is a place.

PART 11 – MISCELLANEOUS AND GENERAL

General duties of LEAs and governing bodies
Sections 175 and 176

Section 175: Duties of LEAs and governing bodies in relation to the welfare of children

332.   This section imposes a duty on LEAs, the governing bodies of maintained schools, and the governing bodies of FE institutions to make arrangements in regard to the welfare of children. LEAs must make arrangements to ensure that their functions in the capacity of an LEA are exercised with a view to safeguarding and promoting the welfare of children (i.e. persons under 18 years of age). Similarly governing bodies must make arrangements to ensure that their functions relating to the conduct of the school, or institution, are exercised with a view to safeguarding and promoting the welfare of children who are pupils at the school, or who are receiving education or training at the institution. All the bodies concerned must have regard to any guidance issued by the Secretary of State, in regard to England, or the NAW, in regard to Wales, in deciding what arrangements they must make to comply with their duty.

Section 176: Consultation with pupils

333.   This section is designed to encourage greater participation by children and young people in decision-making within schools. It places a duty on LEAs and the governing bodies of maintained schools, in the exercise of their functions, to have regard to any guidance (in England from the Secretary of State, in Wales from the NAW) about consultation with pupils in taking decisions affecting them. Any guidance issued must provide for pupils' views to be considered in the light of their age and understanding.

Education and training outside schools
Sections 177 to 178

334.   These sections reflect the fact that education is increasingly being delivered in more than one setting, particularly in respect of vocational training in the workplace

Section 177: Meaning of "secondary education"

335.   The definition of "secondary education" in section 2 of the EA 96 includes education received partly at a school and partly at another institution, such as a FE college. This section extends that definition to include education or training which is provided partly at any other kind of establishment. That would ensure that mixed education provided partly at a school and partly at, for instance, a workplace is treated as secondary education. The section also amends the definition of secondary education so as to make it clear that it includes vocational, social, physical and

recreational training. In this respect the definition of secondary education is brought into line with the definition of FE. Additionally, the section provides for the Secretary of State, or the NAW, to modify certain aspects of the Education Acts to take account of the fact that some pupils may be undertaking part of their secondary education away from a school or college.

Section 178: Training and education provided in the workplace for 14 to 16 year olds

336.   Section 5 of the LSA enables the LSC to fund education or training at an FE sector college for pupils in the final two years of compulsory schooling. This section extends that to enable the LSC in England to fund education or training for such students provided at the premises of an employer in England.

337.   The section also extends the age range for Ofsted / Adult Learning Inspectorate (ALI) area inspections from 16-19 to 14-19 in England and Estyn area inspections from 16 plus to 14 plus in Wales. An area inspection is an examination of the provision of education in a specific locality which results in a report to the LSC. The ALI is a government body that inspects all publicly funded work-based training for people over 16.

Section 179: Rights of entry in relation to inspections

338.   This section amends the right of entry for school inspectors, which is at present limited to the premises of schools, by extending it to include other premises where schools have arranged for educational provision to be made for pupils aged 14-16.

Section 180: Inspections of LEAs: rights of entry etc.

339.   Section 40 of the EA 97 makes provision about the rights of entry of inspectors carrying out inspections of LEAs under section 38 of that Act and their rights to inspect documents. This section substitutes a section for the existing section and in doing so extends these new rights of entry and inspection.

340.   Among the LEA functions which are subject to inspection under section 38 is the arranging of education otherwise than at school for children who, for whatever reason (such as illness, injury, behavioural problems or exclusion from school), would otherwise not receive suitable education. This duty is imposed by section 19 of the EA 96.

341.   The existing section 40 limits the right of entry to premises of the LEA being inspected and schools maintained by that authority. The new section 40 provides for that right of entry to be extended to other premises (under section 19 of the EA 96) on which education is being provided under

arrangements made by the LEA (other than private houses).

342.   The right of entry is accompanied by rights to inspect and copy records and documents including, by virtue of section 42 of the SIA, computer records. These powers are to be backed up by an offence of wilfully obstructing an inspector who is seeking to exercise any of the rights granted by this section.

Allowances in respect of education or training
Sections 181 to 185

Section 181 and 182: Allowances in respect of education or training; learning agreements

343.   These sections enable the Secretary of State or the NAW to make regulations which would entitle people to receive a regular maintenance allowance if they are taking part in secondary education, FE or training. Payments of this type would be similar to the system of Education Maintenance Allowances now being piloted in some parts of England. The current system of payments is on a discretionary basis.

344.   Regulations may, in particular, provide for: the size of payments; income tests to determine eligibility; how long payments can be made for and the establishment of appeals mechanisms.

345.   A learning agreement is defined as a document which sets out certain conditions which relating to attendance at a school, college or training centre; good conduct; and production of assignments. Regulations may make it a necessary condition for receiving a regular maintenance allowance that the student should have signed a learning agreement. The regulations could also require that maintenance payments are stopped if the student fails to comply with the terms of the agreement. The regulations would be able to prescribe both the form and content of learning agreements.

Sections 183 to 185: Transfer of functions relating to allowances under section 181; Delegation of functions relating to allowances; Supplementary provisions relating to transfer or delegation of functions

346.   These sections enable the Secretary of State to transfer any functions arising from regulations made under section 174 to the LSC, or to an LEA. Such functions might include the making of payments, assessment of eligibility and general administration of the scheme. The NAW will similarly be able to transfer functions to the NCETW, or to an LEA. If functions are transferred in this way, the Secretary of State or the NAW may issue binding directions about how the function is to be exercised.

347.   Arrangements may also be made to delegate functions arising from

regulations to any other person or body. The Secretary of State or the NAW may establish appeals mechanisms for decisions about transferring or delegating these functions. The section also enables the Secretary of State or the NAW to contribute towards the costs of any body exercising functions in relation to these maintenance payments.

Student Loans
Section 186

Section 186: Student Loans

348.   This section gives the powers to set in place arrangements to pay off the student loans of any person who meets eligibility requirements to be specified in regulations.   It provides the basis for the Government to implement plans to pay off, over time, loans (including any interest accrued) for new teachers in shortage subjects in schools maintained by LEAs, non-maintained special schools, CTCs, CCTAs, Academies, colleges in the FE sector, non-FE sector specialist colleges in receipt of funding from either the LSC or the NCETW, and Higher Education institutions that offer FE courses.

349.   The section provides a power for the Secretary of State to reduce or pay off any outstanding student loans which a person who is eligible under the proposed scheme may have. The section gives the power to write off or repay any loans made to English or Welsh domiciled students under the Education (Student Loans) Act 1990 (mortgage style loans) or the THEA (income-contingent loans). It also gives the power to repay loans received under any other arrangements, including loans entered into outside England and Wales.

350.   The section gives the Secretary of State the power to determine that any functions under the relevant regulations should be exercised by another person or body on her behalf. It also provides that regulations made under this section should be made by the Secretary of State rather than by the NAW, as student support matters are not devolved to Wales.

Education Action Zones
Section 187

Section 187 and Schedule 15: Education Action Zones

351.   This section introduces Schedule 15 which amends provisions of the SSFA relating to EAZs. It adds to the schools that are eligible to participate in EAZs, to include nursery schools, PRUs and independent schools. These additional types of schools can only participate in EAZs with the consent of the Secretary of State.

352.   The Schedule inserts a new section (11A) into the SSFA to give an

EAF (the corporate governing body) a limited power to amend its governing instrument with the consent of the Secretary of State. EAZ schools and the Secretary of State will still retain the right to appoint members onto the EAF.

353.   The Schedule inserts new sections (11B and 11C) into the SSFA to enable an EAF to add or remove a school from the EAZ, subject to the consent of both the Secretary of State and the governing body of that school.

354.   The Schedule requires the EAF to notify the Secretary of State of any amendments made to its governing instrument. This Schedule also requires the EAF to provide any member of the public with specific current information about the EAF, particularly the names of the EAZ schools and partners and individuals on the EAF.

355.   The Schedule amends section 12(1) of the SSFA, which defines the objects for which EAFs are established. An additional broader educational object is added to allow other educational activities to be carried out subject to the consent of the Secretary of State. This allows EAZs to link closely to other programmes such as those designed to improve nursery education or improve access to HE.

356.   The Schedule ensures that amendments which have previously been made to the instruments which establish and govern EAZs and their EAFs are preserved. The section allows for an EAF to include one or two representatives of the Secretary of State unless she chooses not to make an appointment.

School Inspections
Section 188

Section 188: School Inspections and Schedule 16

357.   Section 188 brings into effect Schedule 16 containing amendments to the SIA. The Schedule amends the duties of the Chief Inspectors for England and Wales to keep the Secretary of State and the NAW informed about schools. The duty in subsections 2(1)(c) and 5(1)(c) to advise about the efficiency of financial management is subsumed within a wider duty relating to management and leadership in schools. This amendment confirms the importance of high-quality leadership and management in the achieving and maintaining of high standards by schools.

358.   The Schedule makes a similar amendment in the duty placed upon registered inspectors in respect of the scope of school inspections which they conduct under section 10. This amendment reflects the coverage of

management and leadership in school inspections and reports.

359.   The Schedule amends section 12 to provide the Chief Inspectors with discretion to use a member of the Inspectorate (defined in section 46 as HMIs and additional inspectors), rather than a registered inspector, to carry out an inspection under section 10, where they consider it expedient to do so. The existing position is that the Chief Inspectors may only do this where it is not reasonably practicable to secure a suitable registered inspector to carry out the inspection. This power will be used to enable inspections under sections 2(2)(b) and 3(1) in England, and sections 5(2)(b) and 6(1) in Wales, to be combined with, or take the place of, section 10 inspections, thereby reducing the number of separate visits by inspectors to the schools concerned.

360.   The Schedule amends the provisions relating to membership of the teams which assist registered inspectors in school inspections under section 10. In addition to inspectors enrolled on the lists maintained by the Chief Inspectors under paragraph 3A of Schedule 3, members of the Inspectorate will be able to act as team members where authorised by the relevant Chief Inspector. This amendment will enable more flexible use to be made of the expertise available for inspection work in schools and will enable some inspections to be combined with the result that the burden on schools concerned will be reduced.

361.   The Schedule amends the provisions in section 16 specifying those to whom copies of school inspection reports must be sent by enabling that duty to be extended to other recipients by regulations. This amendment provides consistency with provisions in respect of schools' post-inspection action plans.

362.   The Schedule amends the provisions in section 17 specifying those to whom copies of schools' post-inspection action plans must be sent. Copies will be required by the Chief Inspectors only in respect of schools for which the inspection report stated that special measures are required or that the school has serious weaknesses. This amendment will remove an administrative burden from other schools.

363.   The Schedule amends paragraph 1 and 2(3) of Schedule 1 to require the Chief Inspector for England when appointing staff, and when arranging for the employment of additional inspectors, to obtain the approval of the Minister for the Civil Service, rather than the Treasury. This change ensures that this provision is consistent with the Transfer of Functions (Treasury and Minister for the Civil Service) Order 1995. The position in relation to Wales, where the requirement is to obtain approval from the NAW, remains unchanged.

Qualifications
Sections 189 and 190

Section 189: Amendments of Part 5 of Education Act 1997

364.   This section introduces Schedule 17, which amends Part 5 of the EA 97.

365.   The amendments extend the powers of the QCA and ACCAC so that their functions in relation to children below compulsory school age are brought into line with those for children of compulsory school age. They also extend the powers of the QCA and ACCAC in relation to qualifications.

366.   The Schedule amends section 23 and 29 of the EA 97. The effect of the amendments is that QCA's and ACCAC's functions in relation to curriculum and assessment for those of compulsory school age are extended to children below compulsory school age.

367.   The Schedule amends section 24(2) of the EA 97. The effect of the amendment is that the QCA and ACCAC can take into account in its criteria for accreditation of qualifications the need to ensure that there are not an excessive number of qualifications in similar subject areas or serving similar functions.

368.   The Schedule amends sections 26 and 32 of the EA 97 to strengthen QCA's and ACCAC's powers under sections 26(3) and 32(3) of the EA 97 by making it explicit that the Authorities can impose conditions after the accreditation of qualifications. It also substitutes new sections 26(4)(b) and 32(4)(b) to extend the purposes for which QCA and ACCAC have right of access to an awarding body's premises. The extension will enable QCA and ACCAC to examine and copy documents in support of their powers under sections 26(4)(a) and 32(4)(a), and, as required by sections 26(5) and 32(5), with the consent of the Secretary of State or the NAW, to limit the amount of examination fees charged by awarding bodies.

369.   The Schedule also introduces new sections 26A and 32A which provide QCA and ACCAC with the power to direct awarding bodies that have failed to comply, or are at risk of failing to comply with a condition of accreditation that may impede the successful delivery of one or more qualifications by an awarding body (or consortium) or that puts at risk the interests of a learner who may be seeking to obtain a relevant qualification. The direction will be for the purpose of restoring compliance with the accreditation conditions and may be used when withdrawal of accreditation is not a viable option. It also amends section 58(6) of the EA 97 to extend QCA's power in this respect to Northern Ireland in relation to NVQs.

Section 190: LEA functions: qualifications

370.   This section clarifies the legal position of LEAs in England and Wales to engage in the award or authentication of educational qualifications. It ensures that LEAs are able to develop, deliver and award qualifications and to charge a fee in respect of those services. The section also enables an LEA to make arrangements with other persons and form, participate in or be a member of a body corporate in order to exercise its powers in relation to educational qualifications. The section is intended to be clarificatory. The powers are therefore expressed always to have been within the powers of an LEA, and are without prejudice to its other powers.

Special Educational Needs: Wales
Sections 191 to 195

Section 191: Regional provision for special educational needs in Wales

371.   There are currently 22 LEAs in Wales, all of which are relatively small in size. The largest has a pupil population of just over 50,000 while the smallest is around 10,000. All the authorities are experiencing difficulties in providing for the full range of children with SEN in terms of the provision required and / or the provision of support services. This section enables the NAW to direct an LEA in Wales, on behalf of a number of LEAs in Wales, to consider whether SEN of children might be arranged more effectively or efficiently by making regional provision. "Regional provision" may be provision of education by a school (a regional school) maintained by one authority for their children and children from other areas, or the provision of goods and services by one authority to other authorities or schools. The LEA must report its conclusions to the NAW. The NAW may issue guidance to LEAs in relation to these duties which those LEAs must have regard to.

Section 192: Directions to bring forward proposals to secure regional provision

372.   The section enables the NAW, by order, to direct an LEA or governing body to exercise their powers to make proposals for the establishment, alteration or discontinuance of schools with a view to establishing a regional school providing for pupils with SEN. A direction may also require proposals to cover arrangements to be made for the provision of education or goods and services by one authority on a regional basis. The school re-organisation element of such proposals is covered by existing statutory procedures set out in Schedule 6 to the SSFA. The NAW may make regulations setting out procedural requirements for proposals for the provision of education or goods / services.

Section 193: Powers of Assembly to make proposals to secure regional provision

373.   This section enables the NAW itself to publish such proposals if it has made an order under section 192 and either no proposals have been made or the time allowed by the order for publication of proposals has

elapsed. It also enables the NAW to make provision for the procedure to be followed for such proposals, which may build on existing procedures set out in Schedule 7 to the SSFA.

Section 194: Welsh LEAs' powers to make regional provision

374.   This section amends provisions in the EA 96 to allow an LEA to establish a regional school or provide goods and services to support pupils with SEN in any part of Wales.

Section 195: The Special Educational Needs Tribunal for Wales

375.   This section introduces Schedule 18, which amends the EA 96 so that SEN appeals that would otherwise be made to the Special Educational Needs and Disability Tribunal (SENDIST) will instead be made to separate Tribunals in England and Wales. At present SEN appeals are made to the Special Educational Needs Tribunal (which becomes the SENDIST from September 2002), which covers both England and Wales. The amendments provide that where the LEA concerned is in England the appeal will be to the SENDIST, and where it is in Wales, to a new Special Educational Needs Tribunal for Wales.

376.   Under the EA 96, regulations relating to the SENDIST are made by the Secretary of State. In accordance with Article 5 of the National Assembly for Wales (Transfer of Functions) Order 1999 (SI 1999/672) they are made with the agreement of the NAW, so far as they relate to Wales. Paragraph 5 of Schedule 18 to the Act amends the EA 96 to give the regulation making power for the Special Educational Needs Tribunal for Wales to the NAW, who also take on the other tribunal functions of the Secretary of State in relation to the new Special Educational Needs Tribunal for Wales.

377.   The regulations relating to the Special Educational Needs Tribunal deal with the procedure to be followed by the Tribunal when hearing cases. The existing regulations under section 336 of the EA 96 are the Special Educational Needs Tribunal Regulations 2001 (SI 2001/600). Regulations also provide for the timetable within which LEAs must comply with tribunal orders (made under section 336A of the EA 96), and the timetable for LEAs to comply with unopposed appeals treated as being determined as in favour of the appellant (made under section 326A of the EA 96). The functions exercised by the Secretary of State include the appointment of lay members of the Tribunal and the payment of the Tribunal's expenses.

378.   Paragraphs 7 to 11 of Schedule 18 amend the Disability Discrimination Act 1995 to allow disability discrimination claims brought by disabled pupils or prospective pupils against schools in Wales to be heard by the Special Educational Needs Tribunal for Wales, rather than the SENDIST. The procedures to be followed in hearing disability claims, or

joint SEN and disability claims, will be set out in regulations to be made by the Secretary of State with the agreement of the NAW.

Other provisions relating only to Wales
Sections 196 to 198

Section 196: Publication and provision of material

379.   This section provides powers over and above the existing, but limited, powers under section 537 of the EA 96.

380.   This section allows the NAW to provide "qualifying material" to governing bodies and LEAs and to require them to provide it to specified persons or to publish it. "Qualifying material" is material which will help parents choose schools for their children, increase public awareness of the quality and standards of education and assist in assessing how well schools manage resources.

381.   It is the intention that the qualifying material which LEAs and governing bodies will be required to publish or provide under this new power will be such as to enable parents and others to measure progress made by pupils while at the school (value-added), and that it may also take into account the socio-economic conditions of the area in which the school is located.

Section 197: Partnership agreements and statements

382.   This section enables the NAW to make regulations requiring any LEA in Wales to enter into a partnership agreement with the governing body of any school maintained by that authority. A partnership agreement will set out how an LEA and a governing body will carry out their functions in relation to a school.

383.   The regulations may, for example, require the agreements to cover the procedures to establish agreed common objectives for pupils' educational progress; the actions which the LEA will take to promote high standards in schools; the actions to be taken to support transition for pupils moving from a maintained primary school to a maintained secondary school.

384.   If no agreement can be reached the LEA has the power to draw up a statement covering how it and the governing body are to discharge their functions. Both the LEA and governing body are under a duty to have regard to the agreement (or the LEA's statement) in carrying out their functions.

Section 198: Transition from primary to secondary school

385.   This is a new power for the NAW to require the governing bodies of

secondary schools and their feeder primary schools to draw up plans together to facilitate the transition of pupils from the one to the other. It includes a power for the NAW to specify in regulations the content and timing of the plans and to give guidance on matters such as the making of the plans or which schools are to be considered as "feeder schools".

Provision of services
Sections 199 to 101

Section 199 and Schedule 19: Transport for persons over compulsory school age

386.   These provisions are designed to give effect to improved planning, coherence and publicity of local transport policies for pupils of sixth form age.

387.   The amendments give LEAs a co-ordinating role in developing policies with key partners to provide effective and efficient transport arrangements for post 16 students. Every LEA will draw up and publish a policy statement setting out the provision of, or support for, transport for students of 16-19 or those completing courses started whilst 16-19. The new section 509AB of the EA 96 contains new criteria that must be considered in devising policies. These are that: no student is prevented from attending FE because of a lack of services or support, choice, costs and the need to travel beyond local LEA boundaries. The policy statement will include provision and support made by schools and FE colleges in the local area. Section 509AA(8) makes it clear that LEAs can make transport arrangements over and above those set out in the policy statement and so allows the LEA and its partners flexibility to respond to changing or unforeseen circumstances where particular cases occur that are not contained in their policy statement. Section 509AA(9) provides that the Secretary of State or the NAW can direct an LEA to make arrangements for transport which are not in the statement. Section 509AC contains definitions.

Section 200: Remission of charges relating to residential trips

388.   Section 457 of the EA 96 makes provision about charging for school activities. Subsection (4) provides for the remission of charges in respect of board and lodging for a pupil on a residential trip where that pupil's parent is in receipt of certain state benefits. The section amends that subsection so as to allow the Secretary of State (or the NAW) to prescribe additional benefits or tax credits that, the receipt of which, will enable the charges in question to be remitted. This flexibility is required to keep pace with changes to the tax credit and benefit system in the Tax Credit Act 2002, and to prevent children's entitlement to the remission of such charges being lost as a result of the changes.

Section 201: LEA functions concerning school lunches, milk etc.

389.   This section replaces section 512 of the EA 96 with three new sections.

390.   The new section 512 is along the lines of the existing provision but makes two changes:

- It enables the Secretary of State (or the NAW), by order, to set conditions that must be met before an LEA is required to provide school lunches. It is intended to use this power to restrict the entitlement to free lunches to those children who are required to attend over the lunch period. Those children who are currently entitled to free school lunches but would lose their entitlement as a result of this change will have their position protected by transitional provisions.

- It extends free school lunch entitlement to eligible children of nursery age who receive education, funded by the LEA, in settings outside the maintained sector. This change will place those children whose parents receive entitling benefits, but who currently are not entitled to free school lunches because their education is provided in private or voluntary nursery settings on the same footing as children educated in the maintained sector.

391.   The new section 512ZA requires an LEA to charge for any meals and milk provided, except as provided for by new section 512ZB. It also unifies the charging regime for pupils and persons who are no longer pupils because they have attained the age of 19 in one provision whereas they are currently dealt with separately.

392.   The new section 512ZB makes the provision of free lunches conditional on a request for free lunches being made by, or on behalf of, a child. This brings the law into line with current practice and ensures that LEAs have legislative backing to resist requests for monetary compensation for the loss of free meals where no application has been made.

393.   Section 512ZB also allows the Secretary of State (or the NAW) to prescribe additional benefits or tax credits, the receipt of which will entitle the parent of a child to request a free school lunch (and, where provision is made, free milk). This flexibility is required to keep pace with changes to the Tax Credit and Benefit System proposed within the new Tax Credit Act, and to prevent the loss of children's entitlement to free lunches (and, where provision is made, free milk) as a result of the changes.

Miscellaneous
Sections 202 to 209

Section 202: Further education institutions: records

394.   Section 202 enables the Secretary of State to make regulations concerning the retention and disclosure of educational records of FE institutions.

Section 203: Further education institution: hazardous material, etc.

395.   This section enables regulations to be made providing for the Secretary of State or the NAW to grant approval to FE institutions to obtain and use specified equipment or specified materials which might endanger a person's health or safety. This section re-enacts provisions in section 218(1)(e) of the ERA and similar provisions for schools are contained in section 546 of the EA 96. FE institutions who obtain approval for the use of radioactive substances or specified equipment under this provision will, like schools, be exempt from registration with the Environment Agency under the Radioactive Substances Act 1993.

Section 204: Baseline assessments

396.   This section removes the statutory requirement on schools to carry out baseline assessments of children. Statutory baseline assessment will be replaced by the foundation stage profile which will be completed at the end of the foundation stage for all children in government funded early years settings (see section 83 and for Wales section 104).

Section 206 and Schedule 20: Nuisance or disturbance on educational premises

397.   This Schedule amends section 547 of the EA 96 ('Nuisance or disturbance on school premises') to extend its provisions to non-maintained special schools, independent schools and LEA-maintained facilities providing instruction or leadership in sporting, recreational or outdoor activities, such as LEA outdoor education centres. Schedule 20 also amends the Further and Higher Education Act 1992 (FHEA) by inserting a new section, which re-enacts the provisions of section 40 of the Local Government (Miscellaneous Provisions) Act 1982 ('Nuisance and disturbance on educational premises') and extends those provisions to any institution within the FE sector. Section 40 of the Local Government (Miscellaneous Provisions) Act 1982 is consequentially repealed under Schedule 22.

398.   These changes extend the scope of the existing provision. They also make a consequential extension of the powers of the police and persons authorised by the relevant bodies responsible for these educational institutions to remove trespassers believed to be committing the offence and to bring forward proceedings against them.

Sections 207 and 208: Recoupment: adjustment between LEAs and special cases

399.   Inter-authority recoupment occurs when a child is educated outside

the LEA in which he or she lives. In these circumstances, the LEA providing the education is entitled to "recoup" the additional costs it faces, in making that provision, from the "home" LEA.

400.   The effect of these sections is to remove the Secretary of State's role in settling disputes between LEAs in England about the amounts to be paid. Current arrangements are retained in relation to disputes between LEAs in Wales. The NAW intends to update the regulations applicable in relation to inter-authority arrangements. Any dispute relating to children who are educated in Wales but the responsibility of an LEA in England will be determined by the NAW, with the agreement of the Secretary of State in England. Where one LEA is in Scotland and the other in England, any dispute which arises will be determined by the Secretary of State.

401.   Section 207 re-enacts, with amendments to give effect to the changes above, section 492 of the EA 96 and section 208 transfers to the NAW, so far as exercisable in relation to Wales, the power to make regulations under section 494. This relates to inter-authority recoupment in relation to pupils permanently excluded from a school maintained by one authority who are being provided with education at a school maintained by another authority.

Section 209: Paid chairmen for local learning and skills councils

402.   Section 209 provides for the LSC to pay the chairmen of local learning and skills councils. At present these chairmen are unpaid. The amount of their remuneration will be decided by the Secretary of State.

General
Sections 210 to 217

Section 210: Orders and regulations

403.   This section contains general provisions about orders and regulations under the Act.

404.   All orders or regulations under the Act are to be made by statutory instrument except for an order made by the Secretary of State or the NAW under paragraph 3(6) or 5 of Schedule 1, an order made by the Secretary of State or the NAW under section 165 in respect of a failure to meet standards in an independent school, or an order by the NAW under section 192 requiring proposals to secure regional provision.

405.   In England, affirmative resolution procedure is required for an order adding to the basic curriculum (section 80(3)), altering the key stages or the core or foundation subjects (section 82(4)(b), 84(6) or 86), amending the areas of learning for the foundation stage (83(3)) or specifying subsidiary

provision in respect of the STRB provisions (125(4)).

406.   All other statutory instruments made by the Secretary of State have to follow the negative resolution procedure, apart from exemptions for schools related to performance, educational programmes under the National Curriculum, assessment arrangements in respect of all key stages, disapplication of pay and conditions orders for teachers in schools in Education Action Zones, or commencement orders, where no parliamentary procedure is required. In addition, if an order is made in respect of teachers' pay and conditions which gives effect, without significant modification, to recommendations of the STRB, no parliamentary procedure is required.

Section 211: Wales

407.   Most of the functions of the Secretary of State under education legislation have, so far as they relate to Wales, been transferred to the NAW by Order in Council under section 22 of the Government of Wales Act 1998 (c. 38). Textual amendments to reflect this have not been made to the legislation. The legislation, therefore, continues to refer to the Secretary of State only, but references to the Secretary of State have to be read, in relation to Wales, as references to the NAW.

408.   Subsection (1) of this section ensures that where the Act confers a new function on the Secretary of State by amending another Act, this new function is exercisable in relation to Wales by the NAW, and references in the provisions concerned to the Secretary of State are read, in relation to Wales, as references to the NAW.

409.   Subsection (2) of this section then ensures that, where functions under any Act have already been transferred by an Order in Council under section 22 of the Government of Wales Act 1998 and an amendment conferring further functions on the Secretary of State is made to that Act by the Act, any powers to vary or revoke the transfer of functions to the NAW also apply to the new functions conferred by the Act.

Section 214: Transitional provisions etc.

410.   This enables regulations made under the Act to make such provision as appears to the Secretary of State or the NAW necessary or expedient for the general purposes, or any particular purpose or for giving full effect to the Act. In particular, they may make provision including modifications for any provision which comes into force before another provision comes into force, or before anything which has to be done under another provision has been done.

411.   Regulations may also be made for amending, repealing or revoking a statutory provision passed before the Act is passed, for applying such provision, and for making savings from any amendment or repeal by the

Act.

Section 215: Minor and consequential amendments and repeals

412.   Section 215 introduces Schedule 21 which contains a number of minor amendments and a number of amendments consequential on other provisions of the Act.

413.   **Paragraphs 13 and 16** of the Schedule repeal sections 23(4)(b), 39, 40, 41 and 42 of the FHEA which relate to the transfer of FE colleges from institutions maintained by LEAs to independent corporations financed by the Further Education Funding Councils now replaced by the LSC and the NCETW. They were introduced to provide new FE corporations with a safeguard against entering into unfair contracts with LEAs with whom they felt disadvantaged in negotiations for transfer of land.   The provisions provided for the Secretary of State's, or the NAW's consent where the LEA was seeking to exclude the transfer of land, or were seeking to enter into a contract, with a third party, to the value of £50,000 or more which would bind the institution in the future.   College governing bodies' experience means they are able to protect their own interests without the Secretary of State's, or the NAW's, support.   Further, these provisions are considered to be obsolete given that there are no longer any LEA controlled institutions to which these sections apply.

414.   **Paragraph 20** amends section 54(1) of the FHEA to correct an incorrect reference. **Paragraph 21** repeals section 60 of the FHEA which serves no useful purpose.

415.   **Paragraphs 31 and 32** correct incorrect references in the Employment Rights Act 1996 to governors.

416.   **The remainder of the paragraphs** make minor amendments consequential on the new provisions in the Act, as follows:

- to the Disability Discrimination Act 1995, Education Act 1994, EA 96, SIA, SSFA and Freedom of Information Act 2000 consequential to the requirement on nursery schools to have governing bodies, and the requirement for nursery schools to be treated like maintained schools for most purposes including the legislation relating to SEN;

- to the Sex Discrimination Act 1975, EA 96, SIA, SSFA and LSA consequential to the changes to school organisation in the Act. In particular as there are now a number of statutory routes which affect school organisation it changes references to the various legislative references to statutory proposals about school organisation to a reference to "any enactment";

- to the Local Government Acts 1972 and 1974, the Disability Discrimination Act 1995, Tribunals and Inquiries Act 1992, EA 96, SIA, and SSFA consequent to the changes made by Part 3 of the Act in respect of school governance, financing admissions and exclusions;

- to the POCA consequent to the new right of the proprietor of an independent school to appeal to the tribunal established under that Act, and to the repeal and replacement of section 218 of ERA;

- to the Public Passenger Vehicles Act 1981 consequent on the amendments in schedule 19 of the Act to education transport provisions;

- to a range of education legislation consequent on the rationalisation of the grant making powers;

- to ERA, EA 96 consequent to the potential changes to KS4 made possible by section 86 of the Act;

- to the Children Act 1989, Police Act 1997, the Environmental Protection Act 1990, the Education Act 1994, the Further and Higher Education Act 1992, the Teaching and Higher Education Act 1998, the SSFA and Criminal Justice and Court Services Act 2000 consequent on the repeal and replacement of section 218 of the Education Reform Act 1988;

- to the FHE 92, EA 96, and SSFA consequent on the repeal and replacement of the STPCA 1991;

- to the Disability Discrimination Act, the Employment Rights Act, EA 96 and the SSFA consequent to the new provisions in the Act about governance;

- to the definition of pupil in EA 96 consequent on the new governing body powers to provide community facilities;

- to the EA 96, EA 97 consequent on the creation of separate National Curricula for England and Wales;

- to the LSA consequent on the changes to schools financing;

- to the THEA consequent on the new provisions about prohibition from teaching etc.

Section 216: Commencement

417. Substantive provisions dealing with five subjects will come into force on Royal Assent. These are the powers of the Secretary of State to form companies, exclusions from PRUs, application of pay scale, student loans and LEA functions relating to qualifications.

418. Section 216 identifies the sections which only the Secretary of State may commence (either because they only apply to England or because they are matters such as teachers pay and conditions where delegated powers have not been devolved to the NAW). It also identifies the sections which only the NAW may commence (because they only apply in Wales). All other sections may be commenced by the Secretary of State in relation to England and the NAW in relation to Wales. Commencement Orders (which do not require any parliamentary procedure – see section 210(5)) may make general or specified provision, different provision for different purposes, and may contain transitional and savings provisions.

HANSARD REFERENCES

The following table sets out the dates and Hansard references for each stage of this Act's passage through Parliament.

Stage	Date	Hansard reference
House of Commons		
Introduction	22 November 2001	
Second Reading	4 December 2001	Vol 376 Cols 189-282
Committee	11 December 2001, 13 December 2001, 18 December 2001, 8 January 2002, 10 January 2002, 15 January 2002, 17 January 2002, 22 January 2002 and 24 January 2002	Hansard Standing Committee G
Report and Third Reading	5 February 2002	Vol 379 Cols 780-835
	6 February 2002	Vol 379 Cols 867-999

House of Lords		
Introduction	6 February 2002	
Second Reading	11 March 2002	Vol 632 Cols 535-648
Committee	2 May 2002	Vol 634 Cols 801-870 and 887-928
	7 May 2002	Vol 634 Cols 995-1015, 1043-1069 and 1087-1135
	9 May 2002	Vol 634 Cols 1284-1340 and 1354-1399
	14 May 2002	Vol 635 Cols 142-218 and 230-280
	23 May 2002	Vol 635 Cols 889-958 and 973-1038
	28 May 2002	Vol 635 Cols 1151-1218 and 1234-1342
Report	17 June 2002	Vol 636 Cols 492-570 and 577-614
	19 June 2002	Vol 636 Cols 741-819 and 842-878
	26 June 2002	Vol 636 Cols 1359-1430 and 1433-1498
Third Reading	3 July 2002	Vol 637 Cols 223-318
Commons consideration of Lords amendments	15 July 2002	Vol 389 Cols 47 – 126
Lords consideration of Commons amendments	23 July 2002	Vol 638 Cols 220 – 261

Commons consideration of Lords reasons for insisting on amendments to which the Commons have disagreed	24 July 2002	Vol 389 cols 1021 to 1043
Lords consideration of Commons amendments to words restored to the Bill	24 July 2002	Vol 638 cols 466 to 478

Royal Assent - 24 July 2002   House of Commons column 1079

House of Lords column 508

ANNEX 1 – ENGLAND AND WALES APPLICATION BY PART

PART	APPLICATION
Part 1: Provision for new legal frameworks	England and Wales except section 13 which applies to England only
Part 2: Financial assistance for education and childcare	England and Wales
Part 3: Maintained schools	England and Wales
Part 4: Powers of intervention	England and Wales
Part 5: School organisation	England and Wales except sections 65 –71 and section 73 which apply to England only
Part 6: The Curriculum in England	England only
Part 7: The Curriculum in Wales	Wales only
Part 8: Teachers	England and Wales except section 139 which applies to Wales only
Part 9: Childcare and nursery education	England and Wales except section 151(1) which is England only, and 151(2) and 154(3) which are Wales only
Part 10: Independent schools	England and Wales
Part 11: Miscellaneous and general	England and Wales except as follows: Section 178 (3), section 179 (2) and (3), section 183(1), section 187 and section 209 apply to England only; Section 178(4), section 179 (4) and (5), section 183(2), sections 191 – 198 and section 211 apply to Wales only.

ANNEX 2 – GLOSSARY OF TERMS AND ABBREVIATIONS

ACCAC — Awdurdod Cymhwysterau, Cwricwlwm ac Asesu Cymru

(Qualifications, Curriculum and Assessment Authority for Wales)

ALI — Adult Learning Inspectorate

CA — Children Act 1989

CCTA — city college for the technology of the arts

CFR — consistent financial reporting

CST — Care Standards Tribunal

CTC — city technology college

EA 86 — Education (No. 2) Act 1986

EA 96 — Education Act 1996

EA 97 — Education Act 1997

EAF — Education Action Forum

EAZ — Education Action Zone

ERA — Education Reform Act 1988

EU — European Union

EYDCP — Early Years Development and Childcare Partnerships

Estyn — Office of Her Majesty's Chief Inspector of Education and Training in Wales

FE — further education

FHEA — Further and Higher Education Act 1992

GTC — General Teaching Council

HE	higher education
HMCI	Her Majesty's Chief Inspector
HMI	Her Majesty's Inspector
IEB	interim executive board
LEA	local education authority
LSA	Learning and Skills Act 2000
LSC	Learning and Skills Council for England
NAW	National Assembly for Wales
NCETW	National Council for Education and Training (In Wales)
Ofsted	Office for Standards in Education
POCA	Protection of Children Act 1999
PRU	Pupil Referral Unit
QCA	Qualifications and Curriculum Authority
QTS	qualified teacher status
RE	religious education
SEN	special educational needs
SENDIST	Special Educational Needs and Disability Tribunal
SIA	School Inspections Act 1996
SLC	Student Loans Company Limited
SOC	School Organisation Committees
SSFA	School Standards and Framework Act 1998
STPCA	School Teachers' Pay and Conditions Act 1991

STRB   School Teachers' Review Body

THEA   Teaching and Higher Education Act 1998

Printed in the UK by The Stationery Office Limited
under the authority and superintendence of Carol Tullo, Controller of
Her Majesty's Stationery Office and Queen's Printer of Acts of Parliament